The truth ABOUT wolves & dogs

DISPELLING THE MYTHS OF DOG TRAINING

TONI SHELBOURNE

Hubble & Hattie

www.hubbleandhattie.com

Hubble & Hattie

The Hubble & Hattie imprint was launched in 2009 and is named in memory of two very special Westie sisters owned by Veloce's proprietors.
Since the first book, many more have been added to the list, all with the same underlying objective: to be of real benefit to the species they cover, at the same time promoting compassion, understanding and co-operation between all animals (including human ones!)
Hubble & Hattie is the home of a range of books that cover all-things animal, produced to the same high quality of content and presentation as our motoring books, and offering the same great value for money.

Please note that, for ease of reading, the text refers to the animals as male throughout, however, female is implied at all times.

Chapter start illustration courtesy Chris Senior

First published in August 2012 by Veloce Publishing Limited, Veloce House, Parkway Farm Business Park, Middle Farm Way, Poundbury, Dorchester, Dorset, DT1 3AR, England. Fax 01305 250479/e-mail info@hubbleandhattie.com/web www.hubbleandhattie.com
ISBN: 978-1-845844-27-1 UPC: 6-36847-04427-5. © Toni Shelbourne & Veloce Publishing Ltd 2012. All rights reserved. With the exception of quoting brief passages for the purpose of review, no part of this publication may be recorded, reproduced or transmitted by any means, including photocopying, without the written permission of Veloce Publishing Ltd. Throughout this book logos, model names and designations, etc, have been used for the purposes of identification, illustration and decoration. Such names are the property of the trademark holder as this is not an official publication. Readers with ideas for books about animals, or animal-related topics, are invited to write to the editorial director of Veloce Publishing at the above address. British Library Cataloguing in Publication Data – A catalogue record for this book is available from the British Library. Typesetting, design and page make-up all by Veloce Publishing Ltd on Apple Mac. Printed in India by Replika Press Ltd

CONTENTS

ACKNOWLEDGEMENTS & DEDICATION

Acknowledgements

I have so many people to thank, so apologies if I leave anyone out. Firstly, Julia Bohanna and Karen Bush for their support, encouragement and technical know-how about writing and the process of getting published. Denise Taylor, Chris Senior, Oliver Matla (www.lupinity.com), Monty Sloan, Patrick Melton, Lee Piper, Emma Coleman, Anne Carter, and many others for their generosity with regard to supplying photos for the book. Also Walkabout Dog Training Club and its clients for letting us invade training sessions to get great shots to illustrate the text.

None of this would have been possible if it was not for the UK Wolf Conservation Trust. Roger Palmer and John Denness, both sadly no longer with us, thank you for teaching me about wolves, but being open enough to take on new ideas. I miss you both. To all the wolf experts who are so open with their knowledge and answer all my queries; special thanks to David Mech and Nancy Gibson from the International Wolf Centre.

Lastly, I could not get away without mentioning my mum, who always believes in me and encourages me in my writing, and everything I do.

Dedication

To all the wolves past and present, at the UK Wolf Conservation Trust.
Kenai, Kodiak, Mika, Alba, Latea & Dakota: run wild and free in wolfy heaven

and

Roger Palmer and John Denness, both now sadly deceased. Thank you for teaching me the difference between wolves and dogs

FOREWORD

by Marie Miller

Many dog trainers and behaviourists attempt to speak with authority on the subject of wolf and dog behaviour. However, their knowledge of wolves is second-hand information gleaned from books, research papers and television documentaries about both wild and captive wolves, much of which is now out of date, and subsequently retracted by those who did the original research.

Ultimately, wolves and dogs are the best teachers when it comes to learning about their behaviour and relationships with their own and other species. While many professional dog trainers work with dogs daily, and have the opportunity to interact and experience a variety of breeds and temperaments, few have the chance to work with captive wolves on the same basis over a number of years. Toni Shelbourne has been in this enviable position, and is therefore able to speak with authority about similarities and differences between domestic dogs and captive wolves.

Readers of this book cannot help but be aware of Toni's passion for both wolves and dogs, and her desire for them to be treated with respect; accepted for who they are as species with some similar traits but also many, many differences. In addition, she recognises that within each species, individuals are just that ... individuals.

Thank you, Toni, for taking the time and trouble to share your experience and knowledge with us all.

Marie Miller
Dog Trainer, Tellington Touch Practitioner & author

INTRODUCTION

Have you ever worked with a dog trainer, or attended a dog training class and felt uncomfortable about the information given? Did you witness something happen to your dog at the hands of the 'professional' which made you squirm? Have you been presented with a long list of dos and don'ts which, you are told, you must follow to the letter because if you don't, your dog will become the alpha in your family? Have you been excluded from a training class, told your dog is untrainable, and made to feel inadequate or a bad owner? Worst of all, did you feel like you were breaking trust with your faithful companion by following these 'rules'?

Maybe, at this point you simply decided not to carry on with the dog trainer's instructions because they just did not sit right with you? And maybe you thought to yourself "That won't work with my dog," only to be overruled by the trainer?

Well, you're not the first ... and you won't be the last.

As a Tellington TTouch Practitioner and wolf specialist, I come across many people who are advised to use harsh methods, punishment, and inappropriate equipment on their dogs as a way of training, supposedly so that they, as owner, maintain their alpha status as leader of the pack. But what if this theory is wrong? Where does that leave us as dog owners? How do we train our dogs without these long-upheld rules and theories about dominance?

I'll tell you: with mutual understanding and respect.

With regard to the dominance theory, if you stop for a moment and analyse the statistics, they do not add up. There are well over eight million dogs in Britain alone, and billions worldwide. How can all of these dogs have dominance issues that mean they challenge their owner for leadership? Compare this to another social species – humans: are we all vying for dominance over one another? Of course, some individuals are stronger, more confident than others: some of us are followers and some leaders. But within our family units, we don't constantly strive to overthrow mum and dad and

IF YOU ARE HAPPY WITH YOUR DOG ON THE SOFA, AND HE WILL JUMP DOWN WHEN ASKED TO WITHOUT SHOWING AGGRESSION, THEN LET HIM ON THE SOFA. HAVING CUDDLES WILL ONLY IMPROVE YOUR RELATIONSHIP. (COURTESY SHANON MCAULIFFE)

HAPPY DOG.
(COURTESY ALI HETHERINGTON)

take control. Parents and guardians guide their children, coach them in life skills, and hold boundary-challenging in check. We don't have to pin children to the floor on their backs to determine their personality type, as some people do with puppies. The alpha role is not evident in any parenting handbooks.

The truth about wolves and dogs will point the way toward free thought, and encourage the reader to first reconsider old myths and misconceptions about their dog, and then question advice given to them by out-of-touch dog trainers. Research shows that the dominance theory existed and the method used in training long before wolf pack hierarchy studies were documented: indeed, in the 1800s it was called the 'Force Method.' A title which says it all, really ...

Although there are numerous dog training books on the market, most either teach how to train dogs using a particular method, or uphold the old dominance theory. *The truth about wolves and dogs* will take readers on a journey of discovery, asking that they reassess everything they thought was correct or have been taught in training. It de-mystifies the confusion and miscommunication between our two species, and explains what dogs really need to be happy.

Your new, rewarding relationship with your dog begins here. I challenge you to throw the old 'rule book' out the window and start afresh, and guarantee you'll be amazed and delighted in the process.

Probably just as much as your dog will be!

Toni Shelbourne

7

DON'T BLAME THE WOLF

This book is not a 'how to' manual, although its intention is to get readers to 'think outside the box,' question long-established theories, and revise out-of-date methods and practices. Over the past two decades of working with dogs and wolves, I have witnessed numerous fads and fashions in dog training, not to mention the advent of 'celebrity' trainers. Sadly, the one method that has endured through the ages is the concept of dominance training.

Progress

Even now, in what is, hopefully, a more enlightened age, I still meet owners who have been instructed to use cruel methods for training their dogs. I hear of many others who have been told to ban their beloved dog from the sofa, or to ignore their pet – who may have been left alone for many hours – when they arrive home, in an effort to establish who is boss. Owners are encouraged to control every aspect of their dog's life; to be the 'alpha.'

Working with wolves for many years, I have come to realise the truth about dog training. Much old-fashioned and incorrect theory exists about how a dog thinks and behaves. Owners and dog training professionals alike have long accepted outdated myths, and are still treating dogs as if they are wolves. As a senior wolf handler for the UK Wolf Conservation Trust, I was often responsible for walking the wolves in our care, and members of the public would frequently ask why they were allowed to walk ahead of their handlers: did that not allow the wolf to take the alpha role? It is often difficult to understand for those who have always been (mistakenly) taught that there are consequences to allowing a dog to think that he or she is boss.

Until a decade ago, I also thought that making my dog wait at the door to allow me to go through first would make me the leader of the pack. Studying wolves since 2001, I have realised the truth: a) your dog is not a wolf, and b) many of the ideas behind dominance training which are attributed to wolf behaviour are incorrect.

Of course, that is not to say that we should throw all of our training methods and good practice out of the window, but we should always know the reasons why we are asking our dog to do something. For example, having your dog sit and wait at the door is safer than letting him charge out, which

A LOWER RANKING WOLF DISPLAYING HER MOOD. EVERY WOLF OR DOG HAS THE RIGHT TO EXPRESS EMOTIONS WITHOUT INHIBITION. (COURTESY OLIVER MATLA)

The truth about wolves and dogs

could be dangerous for him and you. The expression that forward-thinking owners and professionals prefer to use in dog training is 'leadership.' In dog training, flexibility is paramount so that you can understand what your dog is trying to convey to you and respond accordingly. Forcing an animal to do something that frightens him, simply because you are the boss – the 'do as I say' approach – may well result in your dog deciding that you are a weak, bullying leader. Would you do the same with a fearful child?

Dominance dog training has to change. Tragically, some domestic dogs are so frustrated, distressed and misunderstood that their instincts take over: perhaps you've experienced this in the shape of actually being bitten by your confused canine friend? When this happens, it's never the owner who is punished, or pays the ultimate price with his or her life for being 'bad,' of course. There are no canine lawyers a dog can go to and explain "I've been abused for years – it was self-defence and I snapped after it all got too much."

Fundamentally, every dog has the right to display his emotions. Even a very submissive dog has the right to retaliate if his owner continues to pin him to the ground, even after he has given all the right signals that say "I submit," but which his owner has failed to recognise. In truth, we have to stop thinking of ourselves as the master race and learn to listen to and respect other species. Once we open ourselves up to this concept it's amazing how the world and the animals around us make so much more sense. Doesn't a dog – and all animals – have the same rights as we do to display instinct and emotion?

A purpose

In today's society, dogs are no longer able to do the jobs they were historically bred for, and, as a result, are under-stimulated and bored with nothing to do, fed on bad diets and kept in isolation. Problems are inevitable.

The latest embryonic thinking in dog training is encapsulated perfectly by the 2010 COAPE (Centre of Applied Pet Ethology) campaign: 'Ask Why. Say No,' which urges owners to walk away from inappropriate training methods. Similarly to humans, all dogs learn differently and at different speeds, yet none will learn well if he is stressed and misunderstood. There are no untrainable dogs, just unimaginative trainers who do not look at the animal as an individual, and plan a training programme accordingly. It does not matter how damaged a dog may be by the human race, the majority can improve if

empathy and the right handling skills are applied. Sadly, there are too few of these special people around, and we cannot save all of the 'problem' dogs.

Neither is this book a guide to training the perfect dog, or one which will apply precisely to YOUR dog and you: there are far too many variables to ever cover all the characters, influences and situations. It is hoped, though, that it will point you in the right direction of thinking in a different way, and questioning what you are told.

When clients ask me what they should do about their dog's behaviour (as six different people have given them six different suggestions), I simply ask what makes sense and will work for them? Would they be happy if a particular training method was applied to them? If the answer is no, then they should not use it. I should think that the majority of people would be unhappy to wear a choke chain or – worse still – a shock collar, so why would they think that their dog wouldn't mind this?

To my mind, the professional's role is not to stride into someone's home and dictate to them that their dog should not lie comfortably on the sofa with them, or must sleep in a cage in the kitchen. If your dog is happy to get down off the furniture when asked, then why shouldn't she sit alongside you, enjoying your companionship and closeness, just as you enjoy hers? It will make no difference to her acceptance of you as her leader, and, if anything will enhance the relationship between you.

If you are a consistently firm but fair, understanding and confident leader, being on the sofa will not make her believe that she can subvert the alpha position. Leadership comes from within, not from what you do or don't ask her to do. The qualities of a leader are more to do with possessing an inner strength and a calm, confident manner, not how often you make your dog sit at the door. Your animal's respect for you will also grow the more you understand each other. A proportion of dogs I see have experienced a simple breakdown in communication with their owner: they are not speaking the same language, and misinterpretation causes issues as a result.

Dog training can never be an exact science as we are dealing with individuals with different temperaments, experiences, and job roles. If you live with a Jack Russell you would not expect him to necessarily do well at retrieving, for example, or protecting a flock of sheep from predators. Those roles are best suited to retrievers and specialised herd protection dogs.

Few dogs are beyond help, which is made possible by tapping into their instincts and being creative and kind in training methods. This is where dog classes can fall short, as it's impossible for trainers to accommodate all the different learning styles, job roles, and motivation within a class of ten dogs who each need a unique approach.

Then there's the matter of human learning styles: even on a one-to-one basis, it's difficult to achieve tailor-made training, which is why the very few

THERE'S NO REASON AT ALL WHY YOU SHOULDN'T LET YOUR DOG ENJOY THE COMFORT OF THE SOFA: IT WILL MAKE NO DIFFERENCE TO YOUR RELATIONSHIP, UNLESS BOUNDARY-PUSHING ISSUES ALREADY EXIST. IF HE WON'T GET DOWN WHEN YOU ASK, WORK ON THIS WITH REWARD-BASED TRAINING. (COURTESY SHANON MCAULIFFE)

(COURTESY LEE PIPER)

good trainers who manage well-run dog classes that tick all the boxes have my great respect.

Over the years I've had to smile sweetly when people have asked me: "You thought you could train my dog, didn't you?" I have to bite my tongue as what I want to say is: "I can train your dog; it's you I can't train." My point is there are so many factors to properly understanding canines, and delivering appropriate and effective training. What is sometimes put about is not necessarily the truth, or even the whole story.

Myth and legend
Somehow, a huge urban myth has sprung up which says that we have to act like wolves, and occupy the dominant position. The main problem with this concept is that accepted thinking about wolves and pack behaviour – the keystone to all dominance-related dog training – is wrong.

In 2008, nineteen prominent wolf biologists published an article about breeding wolves, and not once mentioned the term 'alpha.' A highly renowned book on wolves, which had twenty-three authors, mentioned the word 'alpha' just six times, and then only to explain that the idea is an outdated concept. So why are dog trainers and owners still using it?

David Mech, one of the world's top wolf biologists, readily admits they got it wrong, and speculates that it takes twenty years for new information to filter down from wolf biologists to dog trainers. We are nearly there – but not quite.

11

Is my dog a wolf?

hounds; homing in on the tiniest detail, be it a lame animal or subtle body language given off by other wolves – or even people in the case of captive animals. Just like our dogs, they can sometimes miss an object right under their noses, however. Dogs have binocular vision that is geared to detect fast moving objects in the distance, not the treat dropped in the grass under their nose!

A wolf howl has the ability to travel and be heard up to ten miles (16km) away, although six miles (9km) is more likely if trees and hills deaden the sound. Hearing small mammals under deep snow ensures an easy meal in winter, after they punch through thick layers with a stiff, two-legged pounce.

Wolves have a very wide vocal range that includes barking, whining, humming, yipping, squealing and growling, and only ever give voice for a specific reason, choosing the most appropriate mode of communication for each situation, which can include tactile communication as well as hearing, body language, vocalisation, and smell. Many myths exist about howling, but wolves do not, for example, howl at a full moon. Howling is a form of long distance communication: reconnecting an individual who is lost with his pack; announcing that a pack is still strong and in control of its territory; inviting others to join a smaller pack to boost numbers; rallying the group for a hunt, and, we believe, for social bonding. When your dog vocalises and becomes over-excited when you pick up the lead, he is displaying a rally call, preparing to 'go hunting' with you!

Adult wolves bark only to sound the alarm if they are frightened, and this can start as a soft 'woof' and work up to a full bark. Cubs bark excessively in their first year as a survival mechanism: if you bark, run and hide you will live longer in a world where everything is dangerous. Other noises can convey anything from aggression and defensive attitudes (low snarl or growl) to submission (whining) or simple curiosity (squeaking). Many believe wolves have a limited vocal range, but this is not the case: in this respect I believe they are far more advanced than dogs. Living primarily with humans, dogs have developed other ways of being understood.

Smell is the wolf's best sense, just as it is with dogs, and they are said to have around 280 million scent receptors. Where people use sight as their first sense to analyse and make sense of the world around them, wolves will use scent. A wolf's nose is constantly active: sniffing out what is around, how others feel, and the sexual or health status of individuals. Dogs apparently have around 120-220 million scent receptors, although a bloodhound has approximately 300 million. Even non-bloodhound types of dogs, in experimental situations, have been able to detect cancer cells diluted to two parts per trillion, so minute that modern machinery failed to register what the dogs could smell.

Like dogs, wolves can pick up changes in body pheromones. They have millions of scent glands all over their bodies which aid communication. For example, scientists think that gender recognition glands are based around the ears, as male wolves sniff this area on females more than on other males. Even raised hackles release clouds of scent for others to read. Strong smells like perfume, fabric conditioner or mint can over-stimulate wolves, and if a peppermint is eaten before interaction with them, they will lick around your mouth or nibble-groom you on the chin.

A STIFF, TWO-LEGGED POUNCE IS USED FOR HUNTING SMALL MAMMALS UNDER DEEP SNOW, AND WOLVES CAN EASILY PUNCH THROUGH SIX FEET OF SNOW TO LOCATE SMALL PREY. THE SAME MOVEMENT CAN ALSO BE USED IN PLAY: HERE, THE WOLF IS CRACKING THE ICE ON THE FROZEN LAKE AND CHASING THE CRACKS AS IT BREAKS. (COURTESY MONTY SLOAN)

All wolves muzzle-greet and hold each other in this area for greeting, bonding or discipline. Adult dogs who want to muzzle-lick are not trying to get owners to regurgitate food (as is often thought to be the case), but are simply greeting or interacting with them. Many puppy-like begging gestures evolve into submissive gestures on maturity, such as pawing, nudging, and rolling on the back. Wolves tend to stop begging for regurgitated food at around eighteen months to two years of age.

The wolf's neck has strong muscles to cushion the vertebrae from the massive pressure inflicted when trying to bring down large prey. Wolves are

HOWLING PERMITS LONG-DISTANCE COMMUNICATION, AND IS DONE SINGLY, AS A DUET, OR IN A GROUP. (COURTESY OLIVER MATLA)

TWO WOLVES TENDERLY GREET ONE ANOTHER WITH A MUZZLE HOLD, REAFFIRMING THEIR BOND. MUZZLE HOLDS WILL ALSO BE USED TO DISCIPLINE, IN PLAY, AND AS PART OF A RALLY BEFORE GOING OUT ON A HUNT, AND IS A COMMON ACTIVITY AMONGST WOLVES. (COURTESY OLIVER MATLA)

often lifted bodily off the ground, thrown, and even flung against trees in the chase. Their legs are straight and long, 'table-topped' under the shoulders and hips and not sloping away; elbows are tight to the chest and turned in, and feet slightly webbed to create 'snow shoes' that allow movement through deep snow that is lighter and quicker than that of their prey.

Wolves are said to be digitgrade: ie, they run on their toes. Massive paws, and big powerful claws help with balance and grip, and only the front feet have dew claws (and never double ones). The dew claws help to rip open a carcass or hold on to bones while cracking and sucking out bone marrow.

Wolves have chests that are narrow and even more keel-shaped than that of a greyhound: I struggle to fit all four fingers of one hand between their forelegs, and my hands are tiny. This shape is helpful in cutting through snow, but I also suspect that it holds all of the internal organs in place more efficiently so they are less likely to suffer from conditions such as gastric torsions. Wolves carry very little fat (although more in winter for warmth), and can utilize food very quickly. A wolf near to starvation can recover condition and weight in days if he receives sufficient food; in the summer he will look very lean as winter fat is shed along with the undercoat to aid cooling.

Backs are straight, lean and muscular, and in summer have an outline similar to that of a greyhound. The average length of a wolf is between five and seven feet (1.5-2.1m) from the tip of the nose to the tip of the tail. Females tend to be slightly shorter in length and lower in height. At their tallest wolves can stand around 36in (915mm) at the shoulder, and weigh on average 70-120lb (32-55kg), although it's not unheard of for wild male wolves to weigh up to 170lb (77kg).

Everything is designed for ease and efficiency of movement: they appear to float over the ground. Wolves can lope all day long at around five to eight miles (8-13km) per hour; their long, strong legs and large paws mean they are built for speed and agility. The forelegs appear pressed into the wolf's narrow chest, with the elbow turned inward and the paws turned outward. This allows the wolf's fore and hind legs to swing in a straight line so that the hind paw falls into the impression that the front paw left. This means only two holes are needed in deep snow, and every member of the pack can use the foot holes of the front runner. With regard to power, think of a dog of around the same size but with at least double the strength. Wolves can easily leap about eight feet (2.4m) vertically into the air from a standing – or even a laying – start, and can achieve speeds of 30-45 miles (48-72kph) per hour in short bursts, which is comparable to a greyhound (the average dog's top speed seems to be 16-31 (26-50km) miles per hour.

Tails are long and straight – never kinked – and have a special gland (the pre-caudal) situated about 4 inches (10cm) down from the croup on the upper side of the tail, which takes the shape of a dark thumbprint with coarser hair growing over it. Scientists are not sure what its role is, but wolves have been observed lifting their tails and rubbing the gland on the entrance of a den, suggesting scent-marking. Whether or not today's dogs still have

THE CLAWS OF A WOLF ARE LARGE AND POWERFUL, AND ARE OFTEN EMPLOYED TO HELP HOLD CARCASSES WHEN FEEDING. (COURTESY PATRICK MELTON)

WOLVES ARE VERY NARROW IN THE CHEST ....
(COURTESY CHRIS SENIOR)

The truth about wolves and dogs

... WHILST DOGS CAN OFTEN HAVE BROAD CHESTS. EVEN THE CHEST OF A GREYHOUND IS WIDER THAN THAT OF A WOLF. (COURTESY LEE PIPER)

IN DEEP SNOW WOLVES WILL OFTEN TRAVEL IN SINGLE FILE, THE WOLF AT THE FRONT BREAKING A TRAIL THROUGH THE SNOW. ONLY TWO FOOTHOLES ARE NEEDED DUE TO THE WOLF'S NARROW GAIT, AS THE HIND FOOT OVERSTEPS THE FRONT PAW PRINT. (COURTESY OLIVER MATLA)

a working pre-caudal gland is open to debate, but an interesting theory is that pheromones are given off when a dog wags his tail, which is why (it is claimed) fearful dogs tuck their tail between their legs to prevent scent being dispersed.

Coat colour in wolves is varied, but ranges from white, black, and grey to red and tawny brown. Must wolves have a facial 'mask' but not as prominent as that of a Malamute, and all have a saddle marking on the back. Undercoat is dense to ensure they can easily survive in temperatures of –50 degrees F (–45C), and even –70F (–56C), and covers everything except the nose – even the inner ear and between the toes is thickly furred. In freezing conditions, the temperature of their feet will be lower than that of the rest of the body to ward off frostbite. In spring the entire undercoat is shed to leave just the coarser guard hair which, over the shoulders and back, can grow to 8 inches (20cm) or longer. This acts as a 'raincoat' all year round, and gives the animal his colour and markings.

Unlike dogs, wolves shed hair in the spring only, and if any part of their coat is clipped out of season, care must be taken not to compromise their ability to remain warm and dry in the colder months, as the coat will not grow

A WOLF'S WINTER COAT IS SO THICK AND WELL-INSULATED THAT THE SNOW WILL NOT MELT ON HIS BODY, EVEN WHILE TRAVELLING. (COURTESY OLIVER MATLA)

back out of season. Undercoat shedding starts at the extremities: legs and ears first, then tail; mammary gland area for females, which sheds early so cubs can find the teats for suckling. Only then does the main shed begin, appearing to work up the body in a line until the spinal area is the only part still with the double coat, though this, too, will eventually shed. The hair comes out in chunks, and the shedding process takes about a month to complete. The

males of some species tend to keep a slight neck ruff, which makes them look bigger and more impressive.

Although wolves can suffer from the same diseases and parasites as domestic dogs, they rarely suffer from conditions like hip dysplasia or other joint problems. Some populations suffer from arthritis, but this is mostly seen in groups that are genetically isolated from other unrelated wolves. Wild

The truth about wolves and dogs

IN CONTRAST, THE SUMMER COAT HAS ONLY THE TOP GUARD HAIR LAYER. HERE, YOU CAN SEE THAT TORAK IS HALFWAY THROUGH HIS SPRING MOULT. HAIR LOSS USUALLY STARTS AT THE EXTREMITIES, WITH THE TOP OF THE BACK THE LAST AREA TO SHED. (COURTESY PATRICK MELTON)

wolves rarely live longer than six or seven years, though can live for sixteen to twenty years in captivity. Having robust immune and digestive systems, recovery from illness or injury can be extremely swift: for example, a serious wound might take weeks to heal on a dog, but just days on a wolf. Even broken bones appear to knit faster.

Our dogs are bred to remain very puppy-like in behaviour and appearance to make them more appealing to people. Wolves become very independent at around five to six months of age, which, in the wild, is when youngsters begin to participate in hunts with their parents and older siblings. Physical maturity is achieved by the time they are a year old and mental maturity at around three years of age; their behaviour is a far cry from the average cute, gangly, playful puppy. At this age wolves can become very dominant in behaviour, especially the males. Offspring leave their parents when between one and three years old to form packs with other unrelated peers to ensure genetic diversity, although juveniles as young as nine months have been known to disperse and survive, demonstrating the speed at which they grow up. From around ten weeks of age, cubs will display hunting instinct, first catching small rodents, then ground birds. Packs are relatively peaceful within their family units but will fight with rival groups over territory. This often results in severe injury or even death.

Given the choice wolves will not inter-breed. Often, a young male will temporarily join an unrelated pack during the breeding season to mate with the eldest daughter, if food and territory are sufficient, as evidenced in Yellowstone Park in America, where wolves were reintroduced. The space and food resources in the park supported an additional litter, allowing the wolves to increase more quickly in number. Joining an existing pack is dangerous and must be handled carefully, although some young males seem to be very sociable, and will meet with several packs until they mature. For example, a radio-collared wolf in Croatia travelled long distances, and interacted with around five or six packs before he died of an infection from an injury that was not wolf-related.

Young wolves under the age of three months seem to readily accept new wolves, after which time the window closes and they become much more suspicious, because, it is theorised, they form lifetime family bonds from this point. Young wolves in the wild may temporarily leave their maternal pack during the summer, returning to hunt in the winter, when adverse weather conditions demand more cooperation for hunting to be successful. Returning family members always appear to be recognised, whilst unrelated wolves are treated with suspicion, and in captivity are difficult to mix together, especially if they are the same sex and therefore in competition for breeding rights. Generally, dogs are happy to socialise with new dogs all their lives, except for some of the ancient breeds which are genetically closer to the wolf.

WOLVES HEAL INCREDIBLY QUICKLY. ALBA, ONE OF THE UK WOLF CONSERVATION TRUST WOLVES, BROKE A VERTEBRA IN HIS NECK IN A FREAK ACCIDENT. HE WAS BACK ON HIS FEET IN FIVE WEEKS AND WENT ON TO LIVE A FURTHER FOUR YEARS. COURTESY PETE MORGAN-LUCAS)

Wolves mate just once a year in early spring, which means their cubs are born into a glut of food as the young of prey animals are also being born at the same time, and are easier to pick off. Additionally, the cubs have time to physically mature and grow thick coats before the next winter. The timing depends on where in the world they live, but in North America and Europe, wolves are usually born around the end of April and into the beginning of May.

Intelligence

A wolf is said to possess the intelligence levels of a four-year-old child, and whether or not this is true, they are certainly accomplished problem-solvers, which is beneficial for adapting hunting strategies, making them more efficient in this respect. Highly independent in nature, if a puzzle is given to a socialised wolf he will never look to his handler for help (in contrast, dogs generally do ask for guidance from theirs).

In the wild these mental skills enable wolves to change tack and learn from their mistakes and observations. They are suspicious, canny animals, notoriously difficult to catch in traps. Their best survival tactic is to fear everything and trust nothing, and wolves will display obvious caution around anything new or different. Ask any wolf keeper about how easy it is to persuade wolves into new areas of an enclosure: it can take months for the wolves to trust a new environment. Objects not in their usual place can cause a suspicious reaction, too: getting a wolf to pass a wheelbarrow that does not usually live on the path to the field is not easy, and they often use me as a barrier to shield themselves from the scary object as they shoot past! When a wolf does approach whatever it is that is worrying, it will always be a lower ranking animal. The breeding pair will hang back and allow subordinates to investigate, keeping a safe distance in case of danger. In wolf society the lower ranking wolves tend to be the more curious, and the higher ranking individuals more reserved and wary: which goes totally against the 'alpha animals always go first' hypothesis that some dog trainers espouse.

Wolves are naturally cautious of humans, and in captivity, if not socialised to humans, will remain wary all their lives. In order to socialise a wolf it is necessary to hand-rear him from an early age, so that he will lose his instinctive fear.

Eating habits

The expression 'wolfing your food' is a fine description of how wolves (and dogs) will eat. A large amount of food can be consumed in a short time – around 20lb (9kg) in a single sitting – and the reason for this is to prevent other predators and scavengers from stealing their kill. Statistically, ravens get more meat from a wolf-kill than the wolves themselves! Everyone benefits from a wolf-kill from the top down: smaller predators such as coyotes and foxes; birds (eagles, ravens, and smaller birds like tits); insects – the dustmen of the world – help clean up the debris, and, lastly even the plants are fed as the nutrients in the blood and carcass seep into and feed the soil (plants thrive over kill sites).

Generally, a kill will be sufficient to satisfy the whole group, but if the pack is too big and food is scarce, it will split up into two or more groups to form new packs, or the younger wolves will disperse earlier than usual. Once a kill

is made, wolves will quickly eat and then cache any leftover meat, often near the den site during the summer so that lactating females can feed without leaving the cubs. Later, if no further kill is made, the cubs will have adequate nutrition.

Adult wolves have no need to eat daily, and will self-regulate food intake to maintain their optimum hunting weight, one reason why you will never see a fat wolf in the wild. Once a large meal has been consumed, wolves can comfortably go three or four days before eating again; a feast-or-famine foraging system. Some dogs will eat huge amounts as quickly as they can if allowed to in emulation of this feeding behaviour, but could well develop problems such as bloat by so doing. The other difference between the feeding habits of dogs and wolves is the latter's ability to eat rancid food (a cache that has been stored for a long time) and not suffer any ill effects.

In some instances canine behaviour is very similar to that of their wild cousins: for example, the way some dogs circle and paw their bedding before settling is comparable to the way that wolves will dig a shallow 'scrape' in the earth or snow, often using their noses to pat plants and dirt in place before settling with their tail draped over their nose to prevent heat loss. In this respect, the coat is so efficient that snow which has fallen onto their backs will not melt, even when they are loping over the landscape or chasing prey.

Body language

Body language in wolves is the same as, if not clearer than that of dogs, and easier to read. They even give the same subtle signals intended to calm certain situations and individuals which, in the wolf world, are called cut-off signals (calming signals with dogs). This is the first whisper of visual communication seen when interacting, and is covered fully in chapter six.

Tail wagging and carriage is used in the same way in both species to show feelings and social standing. It can mean "I'm happy to see you," "I'm about to put you in your place," or even show nervousness. Sadly, many misinterpret the wag of a dog's tail as an indication that he is relaxed, and then are very surprised if bitten: a tail that is held low and moved slowly, or a fast, tight wag can both mean the opposite, in fact.

The behaviour and body language that dogs display is bigger, bolder and easier to read in wolves. Sometimes dogs appear confused, with indistinct or conflicting body language and communication signals, which may result in our misunderstanding what it is the dog is trying to say to us (this mainly occurs when dogs have been punished for displaying emotion). Plenty of dogs show some anxiety at being patted on the top of their head but do nothing about it, apparently prepared to grin and bear our impolite behaviour. It might take an abused dog days, weeks or even months to reach the point where he can no longer bear the treatment he receives, and he retaliates. Others in the same situation may withdraw into themselves as a way of escaping their torment.

A wolf will wait about a nanosecond for inappropriate behaviour to cease before he tells you off, and will be sharp, fast and sometimes unforgiving of inexperienced handlers, or occasionally those in which he senses a weakness. However, if a deep bond exists between you, wolves can be the most affectionate and trusting of creatures. I have often nursed sick or injured wolves on my own with no restraining lead; as long as I respond to their

The truth about wolves and dogs

THE AUTHOR WITH DUMA AND DAKOTA, WOLVES FROM THE UK WOLF CONSERVATION TRUST, ENJOYING SOME DOWN-TIME. (COURTESY DOMINIC ELDRED-EARL)

signals appropriately I am able to administer medications that some dogs would not be happy for me to apply.

Over the thousands of years that dogs have lived alongside mankind they have successfully learnt to understand us, reading our facial and body movements like a book. They have given up a lot to live with modern man, and are now so closely linked with us that they have sacrificed the ability to survive long-term in the wild without us. One example of this is that when a dog bitch becomes pregnant and gives birth, the sire and other pack members are unlikely to remain to help her raise the pups, as would be the case with a wolf birth. She would have to be an exceptional mother to manage entirely on her own – or have human help to rear her young.

Over time we have adapted and designed dogs to fit us and our world, and it should be strongly emphasised that they are separate to and different from wolves. We do not look to the ape world to show us how to teach our children how they should behave: although you may witness primates performing complex tasks which seem very familiar, we would never blame our children's behaviour on this ancient evolutionary link.

We must afford our dogs the same courtesy of treating them as the species they are, and not as wolves in dog's clothing ...

MAI AND MOTOMO AT THE UK WOLF CONSERVATION TRUST (UKWCT). (COURTESY LEE PIPER)

THE AUTHOR WITH DAKOTA AT A MEET-AND-GREET SESSION AT A NATURE CENTRE. DAKOTA IS RELAXED AND TRUSTING ENOUGH TO LAY DOWN, AND EVEN TAKE A NAP. CLEARLY, SHE IS VERY COMFORTABLE WITH HER HANDLERS AND THE SURROUNDINGS. (COURTESY PETE MORGAN LUCAS)

THE MYTHS,
LEGENDS AND
HISTORY OF DOG
TRAINING

The truth about wolves and dogs

Dogs have clearly been utilised by man – and therefore trained – for thousands of years, although the training methods used are now mostly lost. The most common benefits of owning a dog were probably the help he could give with guarding, hunting, and protection during warfare. Much has been written about the Romans, Greeks, Spartans, and the Mongolian Genghis Khan, who all used dogs to fight alongside them, guard supplies, and warn of approaching enemies. Dogs were even employed on the frontline until the First and Second World Wars, and today guard military installations and scent-detect bombs.

Training

Where did training methods and ideas originate? My theory when I began researching the topic of this book was that the study of wolf packs and how these operated was applied to training the domestic dog. To check this hypothesis I read numerous books and talked to dog trainers and owners about why they perform certain actions with their dogs.

After copious amounts of research I concluded that dominance training methods seem to have originated in the 18th and 19th centuries – if not earlier – and long before biologists studied wolf behaviour. I sourced and read books on animal training to gauge how far we have developed over the years: the oldest of which were mostly published in the 1800s.

War dog

The prevalence of harsher methods of dominance training is attributed to the First and Second World Wars, but, strangely, I found the reverse to be true. The head of the British War Dog School – Lieutenant Colonel E H Richardson – wrote in his book *British War Dogs, their Training and Psychology* that he preferred people who had not worked with canines previously as they had stronger bonds with the messenger dogs, and worked in a kinder fashion. These amazing animals had to work independently over several miles, from the frontline to headquarters, negotiating shellfire, bomb-ravaged terrain, and snipers, to reach their keepers. They struggled back, despite gas and shell injury, such was their drive to reunite with their people. A very strong bond was necessary in order for the dogs to carry out the work required of them, and training used habituation and reward-based methods. In my opinion, if a dog was cruelly treated, it's unlikely that he would have returned time and time again to a keeper who treated him badly. I did not read of any really harsh methods for the training of sentry dogs, either, which appeared fairly similar to training methods used for today's military dogs.

Lieutenant Richardson writes:

"Complete confidence and affection must exist between dog and keeper, and the man whose only idea of control is by coercion and fear is quite useless. I have found that many men, who are supposedly dog experts, are not sufficiently sympathetic, and are apt to regard the dog too much as a machine. They do not study the psychology of their charges sufficiently. Another type of man to avoid is one who has trained or bred a few dogs, and thinks in consequence that he knows all there is to know. This unteachable attitude disqualifies a man at the outset. Some of the most successful keepers, that is to say, those who obtained the best results from the dogs

DOGS WERE IMPORTANT TO THE ROMANS. THIS SKELETON OF A DOG WAS FOUND ON AN ARCHAEOLOGICAL DIG BY READING UNIVERSITY IN THE ROMAN TOWN OF SILCHESTER. THE DOG HAS CLEARLY BEEN LAID OUT FOR BURIAL. (COURTESY THE SILCHESTER TOWN LIFE PROJECT, READING UNIVERSITY)

in the field, and were also the most helpful when under instruction at the school, were those who, having a natural love of animals, had had no previous experience of a particular nature with dogs."

He continued in regard to the training of messenger dogs:

"It is easy to understand, therefore, that the messenger dog has to be trained in such a way that it takes keenest delight and pride in its work. The highest qualities of mind – love and duty – have to be appealed to and cultivated. Coercion is of no avail, for of what use would this be when the dog is two or three miles away from its keeper? In fact, it may be said that the whole training is based on appeal. To this end the dog is gently taught to associate everything pleasant with its working hours. Under no circumstances whatever must it be roughly handled or roughly spoken to. If it makes a mistake, or is slack in its work when being trained, it is never chastised, but is merely shown how to do it over again. If any of the men under instruction are observed to display roughness or lack of sympathy with the dogs, they should be instantly dismissed, as a promising young dog could easily be thrown back in his training, or even spoiled altogether by sharp handling."

Force method

It would appear that harsh training methods have been around for well over 200 years. The term 'breaking-in an animal' has been widely used by both dog and horse trainers, and there's no mistaking the intention behind such brutal language, which I find abhorrent. In the 1800s, it was called the 'force method,' and was obviously developed years before the 1940s research on wolf pack hierarchy carried out by Rudolph Schenkel.

One book written in 1895 claims to be kind, as it advocates the force method without the use of the whip, although, apparently, it was fine to use a corncob with nails through it to teach a dog to have a soft mouth for gundog work. Prong or force collars (collars with metal spikes which faced inward) were used to discourage frustrated and bored dogs who were chained up for hours from dragging their kennel around the yard, as well as teaching heelwork by discouraging the animal from walking in front of his handler.

In *Modern Training & Handling*, by B Waters, published in 1894, there's a chapter on 'Instruments Used in Training: Their Uses,' in which Waters refers to prong collars as 'spike collars:'

"The spike collar has been the subject of the most unqualified praise and most unqualified condemnation; it has been claimed that it is applicable and efficient in every branch of a dog's education, and the most extravagant quickness and perfection of results have been ascribed to its use. Much can be said for and against it, not from any inherent virtues or vices in the collar, but accordingly as it is used skilfully or otherwise. Unquestionably, men of uncontrollable temper and vicious propensities inflict terrible torture, and sometimes maim or destroy the dog with it, yet it is only a means to their brutality; in its absence, the whip or boot would more than probably take its place. For such men the collar is wholly unfit as a useful instrument in training, and the men are wholly unfit for trainers. Even in the hands of a novice whose temper and intentions are the kindliest, a great deal of unnecessary pain is inflicted from imperfect knowledge of methods and dog nature, awkward manipulation, and from failure to note the painful effects of punishment. The writer has seen the lesson abandoned and the most disgraceful barbarity exhibited from loss of temper. Such is not dog training in any sense of the term; and the vicious temper of the trainer cannot be ascribed to the properties of the collar. When used merely to gratify such temper, it ceases to be an instrument of education; and ill-natured punishment should not be confounded with training. The great error lies in assuming that any man can take a spike collar and apply it to training purposes without prior experience. No man can use it properly in the beginning."

This is a pertinent observation which can be equally applied to the use of electric collars today, as well as the prong collar that, unfortunately, is still legal in some countries. However, Waters then lets himself down by going on to say that "the whip is indispensable in dog training," though, to his credit, does add: "Dog training can never be reduced to a system of arbitrary rules. With many of the exact sciences, a theoretical knowledge may be exact so far as it goes, but in dog training there is always an unknown and variable quantity which governs the application of the training, namely, the disposition and intelligence of the dog. While a trainer may have an extensive theoretical knowledge, he must learn how to modify or extend his methods by actual experience. No science of training can supplant experience; they are mutually dependent. No two dogs have precisely the same degree of intelligence or the same habits, inclinations, disposition, etc, hence a certain course of education which might be eminently successful in one instance might be ruinous in another. While the system herein taught will serve to train any dog which is capable of being trained, the success depends on the manner of applying it. The amateur cannot expend too much pains in studying dog character, and

thereto he must gain and hold the affections of his dog, otherwise he cannot succeed."

I could not agree more with this last statement: no two dogs are the same and therefore no two problems can be dealt with in exactly the same way.

Waters noted at this time (late 1800s) that the term 'breaking' was slowly being replaced by 'dog training.'

Sadly, others were not as enlightened. In 1865, Major General W N Hutchinson stated in his book *Dog-Breaking*:

"Unlike most other arts, dog-breaking does not require much experience; but such a knowledge of dogs as will enable you to discriminate between their different tempers and dispositions (I had almost said characters), and that they vary greatly is very advantageous. Some require constant encouragement; some you must never beat; whilst, to gain the required ascendancy over others, the whip must be occasionally employed."

Clearly, dogs were not considered to have either personalities or feelings. The only good thing about this book is that it recommends using the older dog to help train pups, and training is advised to begin at just a few weeks, not after the pups have been left isolated in a yard or cellar for months, as many over books suggest.

Books on training of this time advised that dogs needed to be dominated and subdued – with the seemingly contradictory advice that affection and understanding were necessary to achieve this objective. Sadly, many of these anachronistic methods linger on into 21st century dog training classes, one example of which is described in *The Amateur Trainer, Force System without the Whip* by Ed F Haberlein, which was published in 1895:

"Quite a number of dogs acquire the bad habit of jumping all over a person, in a playful way, which is most disagreeable to both the master and his friends. The latter are not spared, unless they make use of boot heels, canes, etc, to ward off too friendly a dog. The fault is easily overcome by stepping upon the dog's hind toes lightly, but sufficiently to cause some pain, the moment he raises up to place his fore foot upon you. A few repetitions will break him."

Couldn't possibly happen now? A few years ago I witnessed a trainer stepping on a dog's hind paws to get him to move back and away from the trainer. Until recently, it was common practice to knee a dog in the chest if he jumped up. Surely, we have come further than this in two hundred years of training?

At least Haberlein got one aspect right:

"The trainer should avoid loud and harsh talk during the exercises. It is unnecessary to give commands at top of voice at close quarters, and if continued, the dog will become accustomed to it, and in the future necessitate loud and louder bawling to attract his attention at all."

When to begin training?

In *How to Train Dogs and Cats* by Frederick H Erb, Jr (published in 1904), we can begin to see why there is still the misconception among owners that dog training should not start until the animal is six months of age. Most of us know that bad habits can become ingrained during this time, and how much easier it is to teach good behaviour from the outset, rather than try and correct bad

The truth about wolves and dogs

habits later on. I am sure we have all witnessed very young puppies learning basic commands at a speedy rate as they readily soak up knowledge and respond to training. This six month myth seems to emanate from the 1800s in relation to gundog training. Frederick Erb advises:

"I always like to start on a dog at six months old, as he is then at the height of his ambition, and can be taught to do anything a great deal easier than when older, and nine times out of ten he will be ready to handle the coveys or flocks of birds he may come in contact with. The best dogs I have ever seen were brought up at that age. Ninety nine men out of one hundred that own dogs do nothing but feed them well and keep them in a cellar or a closed yard for a year, then ask some handler to train their dogs. Oft the dog goes, scared to death the minute he is put in the box for shipment until the handler gets him. Now, what does the handler do? The only thing for him to do is to pet and try to make friends with him. No success; let him loose and he runs off, and you can't help but say the handler is up against a hard proposition. But, if the owner would get off his pup at six months to the handler, or take the pup out walking so he would get used to seeing things, it would take all the cowardice out of him. Look at horses at one and two years old making world records! They are not shut up in a box-stall and not let out, but are given plenty of good exercise and are petted, and this is the way dogs ought to be treated."

Was this the beginning of the socialisation theory?

In his book of 1909, *Hunting Dogs*, Oliver Hartley's method for preventing puppies from chasing livestock advises:

"Let him begin to follow you when he is three or four months old; take him through herds of sheep and cattle, and if he starts after them, scold him; if he continues chasing them, whip him. I do not believe in whipping where it can be avoided, but if compelled to, do not take a club or a number 10 boot, but a switch; and I never correct a dog by pulling his ears for fear of hurting his hearing, as a dog that is hard of hearing is not an a No 1 dog."

Well, that's good to know. We wouldn't want deaf dogs from ear pulling, now would we ...?

S T Hammond, in his 1882 book *Practical Dog Training: or Training versus Breaking*, states:

"Having selected our pup, we will take him home when he is six to eight weeks old."

The criteria for when a pup can be taken from his dam and littermates appears not to have changed even today, but is it the best time? As puppies learn so much from their mother and other dogs, remaining longer with their dam and siblings, whilst experiencing a strong link with people, could well be more beneficial. When we take home our eight-week-old puppy, the chances are he will then be isolated from other dogs and socialisation with them will cease until his vaccination course is complete. At this point, the window for socialisation is almost gone and the pup enters a natural fear period where anything and everything may scare him. Taking him out and about we then question why he is frightened!

Is it simply tradition and economics that dictate we must separate puppies from all they have known at such a tender age, when wild puppies remain with their family for at least a year?

The first lesson, Hammond opines, should be for the pup to learn to 'leave,' which should be taught first in his pen, a distraction-free environment. Hammond mentions habituation in the form of having rabbits and cats close to the puppy so that he will learn to leave them when hunting.

Talk to your dog

Hammond continues with conversing with your dog:

"You should also talk to him – not baby talk – but use intelligent, rational language, just such as you would use in talking to a ten-year-old boy, and you will be surprised to see how soon he will understand your conversation. We are well aware that many persons will ridicule this, and will claim that a dog should be taught just as little as will answer to make him understand his duties while in the field, and that what they term 'fancy training' is a positive injury to his usefulness. We have no sympathy with these views."

The dog world is still divided on this subject: some suggest that only one word commands be used, whilst others contest that their dog understands every word they say. My experience is that it's possible to talk to dogs in sentences; they are intelligent enough to pick out the words they need to understand what it is you're saying. On more than one occasion I have asked a dog to put his toys away in the toybox and he has done so!

Those within the more holistic training world of Tellington TTouch Training and other methods, know that the power of intent is very strong. For example, how often does your dog disappear and hide when your intention is to take him to the vet, but come running to have his lead put on for a walk in the park? Talking allows humans to picture what they want and dogs are really good at picking up on this. It may also be that we are more focused on what we want them to do. When training dogs in ground work and leading exercises, I often ask "Can you take one step for me?" It's amazing how often they do.

An indisputable fact is that puppies, like children, have very short attention spans, so benefit more from short, frequent training sessions rather than one long one. Even in 1882, Hammond observed:

"The shorter the time occupied in his lessons at this tender age [young puppies] the better."

Even adult dogs find it hard to concentrate for more than twenty minutes at a time (about the same as human adults!).

Compliance at all times?

Hammond also noted that:

"Short lessons are important, but don't take him away from a bone or play if he is engaged with it until he is finished, however, if you do give a command make sure he does do it."

The notion of making a dog obey at all times and not letting him get away with anything, clearly came about much earlier than the alpha wolf theory. On numerous occasions, I have had to explain to students observing wolves that just because a higher ranking wolf has allowed a prize to be taken from him, it does not mean that he is losing his status. It is often noted in both dogs and wolves that play items are sometimes presented to another animal in order to initiate play.

Sometimes, if a higher ranking wolf is not hungry, he will allow others to take food: do we not do the same with our children? Let them win a game, or have a piece of our cake if they ask? Why would canines be any different? And if our children do not take advantage of this leniency, why would our dog? Of course, there will be boundary pushing – it's natural in every species – but how we deal with it is what counts.

Many people have unruly children, and that old adage 'Give them an inch and they will take a mile' is as true for people as it is for dogs. We frequently blame our pets for our own weaknesses. When a dog's bad behaviour is described to me, my response is often "Well, don't accept it." It's as simple as that. If your dog goes mad when you pick up his lead, simply sit down and wait for him to become calm, and repeat as often as required to achieve your goal. It may take a few days for your dog to learn that in order to get what he wants – in this case, a walk – he must wait calmly and patiently. Consistency is the key here.

Heelwork

It's sometimes assumed that teaching your dog to walk to heel is only possible if the owner holds the alpha position, but wolves do not follow this rule. A wolf mother and father are generally the ones who decide when it is time to go out hunting – as with our own families – but if another wolf is better at tracking, he or she will take the lead. In addiiton, the entire pack may also share the task of breaking a trail through the snow. The notion that dogs must walk by our side again seems to have originated from the gundog training world. S T Hammond's *Practical Dog Training: or Training versus Breaking* seems to provide a clue to this:

"When well accustomed to the restraint of the chain, he should be taught to come to heel and quietly walk by your side. We greatly prefer that our dog should keep this position with his head just opposite our legs, where we can see him without turning around, instead of having him behind us."

Can the reason for this rigid formation really be that simple; a way of being able to see where your dog is without turning round?

Types of training

By the early 1900s, scientists such as Edward Thorndike and Ivan Pavlov were beginning to prove their theories about learning, and identifying methods such as 'classical' and 'operant conditioning.' Even if these phrases are unfamiliar, many people will have used these methods to train their dog. Often, dogs are taught to toilet on command using a key word or phrase ('hurry up') to elicit a classical training response: ie, the word stimulates the action. Operant conditioning is used to clicker train: our dogs will run through many actions to find the one we want, learning by trial and error as well as positive association.

Over the last few decades, modern-thinking trainers have used these theories to full advantage in an effort to change existing, antiquated methods. I believe that it will be our temperaments which will dictate the path we choose to follow with our dogs: happily, more and more people seem to be choosing a more holistic approach to training and living with their dog, the result being that they better understand their animal's behaviour, and make allowances for

the pressures that modern living imposes on him. The tide is slowly turning, and terms like alpha are used less and less. In a hundred year's time, will that word still be in use? I hope not.

Current views and opinion

However, when talking to dog owners and trainers, the term alpha still crops up. Owners talk about being the alpha, or tell me that their dog is dominant. On investigation, these so-called 'dominant' animals rarely are. In my experience very few pet dogs are truly looking to be 'top dog.' Yes, some may be pushing boundaries if their owner allows them to, but few take this to true leadership of the household. It's more often the case that his frustration with being constantly misunderstood is behind the unwanted behaviour.

It's interesting how language works, and understanding and interpretation can be quite different. We change how we perceive language to correspond

The truth about wolves and dogs

with what we want to hear, or misunderstand the initial response. Years ago, when working for Guide Dogs for the Blind as a kennel staff member, I regularly witnessed dogs acquiring bad reputations. If a trainer deemed a dog to have a certain trait or fault, this would stay with the animal until others – who had never even worked with the animal – could be heard commenting about these 'faults.' If the first trainer was wrong in their assessment, ultimately, the dog became labelled as difficult and suffered for that.

It's the same with training methods. The founder of a training method will have their work interpreted by others, often incorrectly, and influence others with their take on the method concerned, which, before long, bears no relation to the original concept.

A contemporary study of how pack hierarchy operates is a good example of this. The evidence from completed questionnaires I had students complete demonstrates that few truly understand the theory or application of the dominance method. For example, most people believe there is only one alpha per group. (Use of the term 'alpha' has been largely abandoned among wolf biologists for the last twenty years: this will be fully explained in the next chapter.) However, a pack always has two leaders: a male and a female (referred to in the wolf world nowadays as the breeding pair).

Owners and trainers sometimes persist with old, 'dominant' behaviour without fully understanding the reason behind the idea. Take eating before your dog, for example. Numerous people eat before their pet, and even mimic eating from the dog's bowl before giving Fido his dinner, in the mistaken belief that, in the wild, the alpha always eat first. I feed my dog when it is convenient, planning her walk and feeds so as not to exercise her on a full stomach. After I've eaten my evening meal, the last thing I want to do is break my relaxation and get up again to feed and walk her. She knows that my food is not for her and pays no attention to me when I eat it. If feeding her first makes her dominant, would she not be showing her dominance by trying to take my food from me?

Another example. The reason why we should go through doorways before our dogs is that this is safer for all concerned, not because we need to prove we are the boss: after all, wolf leaders do not always lead their pack from the front.

Conclusion

Like us, dogs fit into many categories, and not all want to rule. All animals – whatever their species – will try and push the boundaries, it's part of life and learning. Teenagers usually try to stay out a little longer each night: if we let them know the consequences of this, chances are they won't try it again. How you deal with that attempted boundary-push is the important factor. Your teenager is not dominating you, he or she is testing you, and dogs may also try this.

Don't run the risk of permanently spoiling the relationship between you by dealing too forcibly with the issue.

MOTOMO AT UKWCT.
(COURTESY LEE PIPER)

The truth about
the alpha

The truth about wolves and dogs

In the 1930s and 40s biologists thought that a wolf pack consisted of unrelated individuals who came together at the beginning of winter to form a group and breed. In those days they did not possess today's advanced methods of tracking and studying wild wolves, and, instead, simulated scenarios in captive conditions, noting down their findings, observing that wolves competed for position, and a hierarchy was formed. This is not dissimilar to a group of people coming together and going through the forming, storming, norming and performing stages of team building. The competition in these captive wolf packs was probably primarily over breeding rights.

In 1946, leading behaviourist Rudolph Schenkel described his findings, noting that there was a dominant female and male in each pack. It was he who coined the terms 'alpha,' 'beta,' etc. His study was conducted on ten unrelated wolves in a 200m square enclosure. The smallness of this space invariably caused the wolves stress, which would also hugely influence the results. Nevertheless, biologists adopted Schenkel's ideas, and it was many years before it was realised that a pack is a family group, with the breeding pair simply bringing up their young.

Raising a family
Like children, wolf offspring are guided and coached by their parents, who ultimately hold authority or 'dominance' over them. Yearlings will naturally help take care of the new cubs, just as human offspring may tend to younger siblings.

Within the pack aggression levels are low. Young adults generally disperse to find mates of their own at between one and three years of age, and, while still with her maternal pack – and only if conditions are right – an older daughter (who reaches sexual maturity at around 22 months of age), may breed, but only with an unrelated male who would have joined the pack temporarily. These 'adoptees' have an important role in breeding, as they ensure genetic diversity.

Family life
There is still much debate about how a wolf pack functions. The idea of a linear structure – alpha, beta, etc – has been mainly superseded by the family unit. Like any family, dynamics can be complex, and cooperation is needed to survive; I believe that our understanding and explanation of pack structure is over-simplified, often in the name of teaching the general public about dog behaviour. Or maybe it's just that we don't understand the social structure of wolf life.

Within our own society, no two families function in the same way: some

ALL PACK MEMBERS WILL NURTURE THE CUBS. HERE, AN ADULT IS ALLOWING THE CUBS TO PLAY ON HER, AND BEING VERY GENTLE WITH THEM, EVEN WHEN THEY CHEW ON HER TAIL. (COURTESY MONTY SLOAN)

are extended by step-parents and step-siblings, whilst in others, unrelated individuals are considered 'family.'

Why should dogs and wolves be any different? A pack of wolves is fluid in its structure: it changes as the wolves age, get sick, or die. As maturing offspring disperse, there is little sexual competition unless the pack comprises more than one mature, possibly unrelated female, who sees a chance to take control of the breeding rights.

In human families, leadership roles change and even reverse over time: children often find themselves caring for parents, making decisions for them, looking after finances, etc, and it's a similar story with wolves. I know of an old red wolf that used to be the breeding male before handing leadership to his children. His mate had died, and an unrelated wolf had teamed up with one of his offspring to form the breeding pair. The old male's teeth were too worn to hunt, so the pack looked after him by regurgitating food for him to eat, as if he was a cub.

Indisputably, wolves show concern for one another, protect and nurture their young cooperatively, and will even raise each other's offspring. In short, they work as a team, each member a cog in a well-oiled wheel, without whom it is harder for the others to survive. United, they are much more likely to thrive.

To again draw a parallel with our own families, within a pack a division of labour is evident. Certain wolves may be better suited to certain tasks: for example, it may be the breeding pair who decide when it's time to go hunting, but tracking may fall to another member who is better at this, and will lead the expedition in finding food.

The experienced wolves will take the more challenging, dangerous roles when bringing down prey. An example of this is the hunting technique known as the 'nose hold,' which requires skill and wisdom to achieve successfully, particularly if a wolf wants to survive longer than the moose he is trying to bring down, as just one kick can injure or even kill him. Younger pack members are encouraged to practice their hunting skills: in a real hunt they may form the bulk of the team, running the prey to tire it before the more experienced adults go in for the kill.

Wolves coach, protect and discipline their young in exactly the same way as we do. The very young are indulged, and get away with 'naughty' behaviour like hanging off dad's tail, or biting big brother's ear. They also get preferential treatment when it comes to food. 'Teenagers' are coached in the skills they will need to survive, and disciplined when they step a little too far out of line.

When 'alpha' is right

In the wolf world the term alpha is now only really used to describe a wolf who has had to fight his way to the top, and wants breeding rights over others of a similar age. In captive packs, when wolves are forced to stay together unnaturally for years at a time, in-fighting may occur and different dominant breeding leaders emerge over time.

The other appropriate use of terminology like alpha and beta is in a pack with additional breeders. David Mech, a world-leading wolf expert, says: "Most packs possess only one breeding pair. Rarely, in such a pack, a daughter remains longer than usual and becomes a breeder, in which case, her mother is legitimately called an alpha female and the daughter a beta female."

The wolf pack

So, to sum up, a pack usually consists of a breeding male and a breeding female, with offspring generally below the age of sexual maturity (usually 22 months). The breeding female, if raising young, spends much of her time tending the cubs and defending them from would-be predators, such as bears. The breeding male is more occupied with food gathering. The breeding female will show submission to the male, but he will readily give up food to her to feed herself and the young before the cubs mature. Once the cubs are older, if the prey animal they are feeding on is large enough, all members of the pack will feed together. However, if food is scarce, the breeding male and female will feed first and then give priority to the current cubs; yearlings have to wait. It is claimed that lack of food at this point may trigger dispersing behaviour amongst the previous year's cubs, but this is unproven.

In the wild, spring is the only time that being able to closely observe wolf packs for a sustained period of time is practically guaranteed, as the cubs are in the den and the pack has to remain in one place. After the cubs become mobile, it's much harder to track the movement and behaviour of the pack.

The truth is we are still figuring out how packs work. Many factors affect this, and different wolf species – of which there are many – will also behave differently.

The human pack

So, how should we relate the foregoing to our relationship with the family dog, and our human/dog pack?

It's important to appreciate that your dog is not a full-blown wolf. Although classed as a sub-species of the wolf, (our pet dog's scientific name is Canis lupus familiaris), as already noted dogs differ genetically by 0.04 per cent. This doesn't sound much but it's enough to make two different species. Even within the numerous wolf species and sub-species, behaviour and social structure can differ. It is more accurate to regard your dog as a diluted version of a wolf, who has been engineered by man to suit the roles we want him to carry out, such as herding, hunting and guarding. Some breeds will exhibit more wolf-like traits than others: independence, wandering, and predatory drive, for example.

Over many generations the dog has gradually moved away from his ancestor. Our domestic dogs never fully mature, and are bred to remain very puppy-like in demeanour and appearance in order to please and be appealing to us. They mostly mix happily with other dogs without signs of territorial aggression, and few show true predatory instincts.

In short, our dogs are not the dominant animals we have been led to believe, and certainly do not need to be bullied into submission.

Myth-busting

I'd like to dispel some of the myths behind dominance training. In a wolf pack a strong leader is calm, quiet, and slightly aloof. He (or she) will command authority with a soft growl, a look or shift in body posture.

The truth about wolves and dogs

DESPITE HAVING SUCH POWERFUL JAWS, WOLVES WILL OFTEN USE CUNNING AND MISDIRECTION RATHER THAN AGGRESSION TO GET WHAT THEY WANT. HERE, TORAK & MAI WOULD LIKE TO TAKE THE RABBIT FROM MOSI, AND ARE USING PLAY TO DISTRACT HER IN THE HOPE OF DOING SO. (COURTESY DENISE TAYLOR)

Bullying, higher ranking wolves within the pack are the opposite: they feel they must constantly show the world that they are in control by picking on subordinates in a very physical way. They dominate in a rough manner – for example, by knocking another to the floor and nipping or muzzle-punching the lower ranking wolf. In captive packs these characters can cause countless problems, ultimately creating instability within the group.

The wolf has numerous ways in which to express himself, governed by complex rules and signals to ensure harmony. An outright fight will be avoided at all costs, and cunning tricks and mind games are used to get what they want from one another. Ritualised aggression occurs daily as part of the family banter but strict rules of engagement generally ensure no harm comes to anyone. This ritualised aggression can seem to the uninitiated to be a full-on fight, but actual wounds will only result if the interaction is over a serious issue, which rarely is the case. Wolves know how far to go, and if one feels threatened or overwhelmed, a signal will be given to cool the situation.

Dogs give these signals, too, but we do not always notice them, or understand them if we do. I have been told many stories over the years about dogs biting owners who have physically reprimanded them, but surely any animal has the right to defend himself if attacked, especially if the subtle signals of submission he's given have been ignored?

An excellent example of this is young wolves playing. They will often practice hunting holds on each other, usually by gripping the underside of the neck of another who is on the ground. Should the hold become too hard, or sustained for too long, the wolf being held will give a vocal signal, and will be instantly released. The sound he gives is quite small but very distinct, and is always respected. It's tempting to speculate that this behaviour between wolves is the origin of the 'alpha roll,' the practise of pinning a puppy to the ground to determine status, on which some trainers are keen.

Wolf play behaviour possesses a subtlety that is often misunderstood. In fact, wolf parents do not often roll their young over and hold them down,

34

although a younger or lower ranking wolf may voluntarily roll over in front of a parent or older sibling as a gesture of appeasement. If this is not felt to be sufficient, the older wolf may follow this with stronger discipline, such as a muzzle punch or nip to the belly, but usually only during the breeding season.

A person who attempts an alpha roll with their dog should be aware that they are placing themselves in a position where they could be bitten. My advice is: do not to attempt it. You put yourself at risk, convey the wrong message to your dog, and show yourself as a weak, bullying leader. Your relationship with your dog will definitely suffer as you will lose his respect and trust, and also seriously frighten a puppy.

Give a dog a bad name is an apt phrase, as dogs are mislabelled all the time. A growl from your dog when you take him by the collar to remove him

from the sofa does not necessarily mean he is trying to be dominant. Ask yourself: did my dog get bowled over in the park earlier; is he in pain, maybe? If you had hurt your neck and were grabbed by your shirt collar in order to move you from A to B, wouldn't you snap?

When going through a doorway, by all means ask your dog to wait, but do it for the right reason: not because it will reinforce your status as leader, but because it's good manners, and safer for your dog to wait instead of rushing out, maybe into traffic.

I was often asked when out walking the wolves whether they were dominant because they were walking ahead of me on the lead, and the simple answer is 'no;' they are just enjoying the walk and taking in the smells and sights. Guide Dogs are not being dominant when walking ahead in the guiding

ANOTHER MUZZLE HOLD, THIS TIME APPEARING VERY AGGRESSIVE. BUT LOOK CLOSELY AT THE TEETH; THEY ARE EXERTING HARDLY ANY PRESSURE. THIS IS RITUALISED AGGRESSION. (COURTESY MONTY SLOAN)

ANY ANIMAL WILL TRY TO DEFEND HIMSELF IF THREATENED. THE WOLF ON THE FLOOR IS OBVIOUSLY FEELING FRIGHTENED AND UNDER PRESSURE – SO IS BEGINNING TO FIGHT BACK. (COURTESY OLIVER MATLA)

THE DOG ON TOP IS PLAYING IN AN EXUBERANT MANNER, AND THE DOG ON THE GROUND HAS ALLOWED HIMSELF TO BE PUT IN A SUBMISSIVE POSITION IN AN EFFORT TO HALT THE ACTIVITY. THIS DID NOT ACHIEVE THE DESIRED EFFECT, HOWEVER, SO THE SUBMISSIVE DOG HAS BEGUN TO FIGHT AGAINST THE IMPOSITION: NOTE HOW HE IS DRAWING UP HIS HINDLEGS TO TRY AND PUSH OFF THE BOISTEROUS DOG. IF THIS DOES NOT SUCCEED, HE MAY HAVE LITTLE CHOICE BUT TO ESCALATE THE FIGHT/FEAR RESPONSE IN ORDER TO EXTRICATE HIMSELF FROM A SITUATION THAT HE REALLY DOES NOT LIKE. THIS COULD ALSO HAPPEN IF A PERSON TRIED TO PIN DOWN A DOG, AND FAILED TO READ THE SIGNALS THAT THE ANIMAL GAVE OFF. (PHOTO EMMA COLEMAN, BLINK PHOTOGRAPHY, TAKEN COURTESY OF WALKABOUT DOG TRAINING GROUP)

WOLVES RARELY KNOCK EACH OTHER TO THE GROUND, BUT OFTEN A SUBORDINATE WOLF WILL ROLL OVER TO SIGNIFY SUBMISSION AND APPEASE A HIGHER RANKING WOLF. THE WOLF ON THE RIGHT IN THIS PHOTO IS ABOUT TO ROLL WITHOUT ANY CONTACT FROM THE OTHER WOLF. (COURTESY OLIVER MATLA)

position, so why should we think our own dog is dominant if he walks ahead at the end of the lead? Usually, a dog who pulls on the leash is either excited to be out, or pulling against the restriction of the lead. Or he may be physically out of balance or not trained to walk properly on a lead.

It's preferable for all if he walks on a loose lead by your side, but this has little to do with pack position. None of the wolves challenged us as handlers just because they walked in front.

. Wolves do not wait for the highest ranking wolf to walk through a narrow space first, and they certainly do not wait their turn when dinner is served, except if food is scarce, as already explained.

The other complaint I often hear is: "My dog is dominant because if I argue or rough-house with my partner, he jumps up and tries to bite or leap between us."

This is actually the sign of a good lower ranking animal – an omega (see right) – whose role it is to redirect aggression by putting themselves between fighting breeding pairs, to prevent injury to the aggressors and therefore possible break-up of the pack. Although we try to move away from using the term 'alpha,' in relation to wolves, it is the case that packs have an omega: the lowest ranking animal, and, in this respect, the term is widely used.

David Mech says: "I see no reason not to use 'omega,' which implies a very low ranking wolf. These do exist and could just be the runt of a litter, for example. They sometimes get picked on, or, in a larger pack, a maturing individual that doesn't want to disperse might be harassed by other pack members."

Omegas are resourceful and often use play to defuse a situation by initiating a game, which gives the lie to another well-worn theory that it must be us who starts and ends a play session.

By all means be your dog's leader, but please think about and question these old myths, especially when they seem to make no sense. Teach good manners, guide and shape behaviour with calm, quiet authority. Remember, nobody likes a bully, and dogs are no exception.

Pack structure and roles: a summary
Role of the breeding pair
In wolf packs the breeding pair's job is to produce and raise the young. To do this successfully they need a territory that they can defend, and assistance from others in the pack to hunt and bring down prey. They will protect their family and each other, and teach their young how to survive on their own. If the cubs are raised successfully, they will be expected to leave home and start packs of their own.

In our society, we do all of these things, too, expecting, in return, a little respect, help around the house and with looking after siblings, cooperation in family activities, and good manners when interacting with other people.

Role of the young adult
Adult wolves support their parents in finding food, guarding territory, and helping to look after the cubs. They provide cooperation, companionship and support in day-to-day life. They will often take turns as babysitter to younger cubs. They are constantly learning from their parents how to hunt and survive.

Role of the lowest ranking wolf: the omega
The lowest ranking wolf may be male or female, and can end up in this role for many reasons. It's not unheard of for this wolf to have once been part of a breeding pair, or to one day rise to that status. Many omegas are happy and pragmatic about their role, and get on with the job.

Theories about the omega's role vary. The majority of scientists agree that his or her main task is to relieve stress within the pack, and act as scapegoat for frustration. As noted earlier, the omega may even insert himself in-between a fighting breeding pair to prevent injury to the two leaders, and therefore possible break-up of the pack. Omegas are resourceful, and will use play to defuse a situation – so can often be seen initiating a play session.

Bite inhibition
The concept of a scapegoat may be difficult for us to feel comfortable with, but what may appear to be extreme wolf aggression and a hard bite is usually harmless, due to the animal's natural bite inhibition. Careful observation of wolves play-fighting will reveal that their teeth do not even touch the skin of their opponent, even though it seems that they are trying to do each other serious damage. If there was serious intent, the omega – or any other wolf – could be killed, but this is rarely the case as a warring, dysfunctional pack would be counterproductive to the pack's wellbeing.

Wolves do often nip, or even bite each other, it's true, but rarely is blood drawn; if it is, you know there's serious trouble in the pack. This happens more in captivity than in the wild, as captive wolves are so often crammed into tiny enclosures with too many others. With offspring who are unable to disperse tensions can run high, especially during the breeding season.

Conclusion
Pack hierarchy is fluid and nothing is permanent. Many factors affect a wolf's standing in the pack, and their personality. Every wolf has the right to leave and strike out on their own. The pack is a cooperative, mutually beneficial structure, a group of individuals who are stronger together than apart. Wolves avoid in-fighting and its inherent risk to health and home. We could learn much from them about how to work together in harmony.

How pack structure and rules relate to the domestic dog
We now know that if your dog jumps between you and your partner when you are fighting he is trying to calm the situation, or redirect the aggression to himself. He is not being dominant but, in his eyes, carrying out a vital role to preserve his pack.

Equally, it's fine to let your dog start the odd play session, as long as it's controllable and he is not constantly attention-seeking. If he wins a few games of tug, this will not generally mean that he will regard himself as boss. Higher ranking wolves often allow cubs to win a game (just as we do with our youngsters), or simply not want an object enough to fight for it and risk injury. If they really wanted it, they would use cunning and problem-solving to achieve this, using play and distraction to obtain what they want. We do this, too, by offering our dog a tasty treat in exchange for something we want.

WOLVES OFTEN SHOW AFFECTION TOWARD EACH OTHER. THEY WILL GROOM, PLAY, AND ALSO LAY CLOSE TO ONE ANOTHER, ESPECIALLY THE BREEDING PAIR DURING THE BREEDING SEASON. (COURTESY LEE PIPER)

And there's no problem with your dog walking ahead of you if it is safe for him to do so and you are in control of the situation.

Love and affection

Wolves are visibly affectionate toward each other, and can often be seen engaging in mutual grooming sessions, or lying close to each other, maybe even touching, especially the breeding pair. Cuddles and affection are just as essential to a dog's wellbeing.

Play is really important. Many dogs are under-stimulated mentally and physically, and become bored and lonely on their own. A daily play session can make all the difference to your dog and your relationship with him. Wolves play throughout their lives at any opportunity: it's vital for group bonding.

Social inclusion is also really important for your dog. If you go to the pub and it's dog-friendly, take him with you! My dog was well-known where I lived: accompanying me to parties, the pub and on trips. Wherever I was, Buzz was,

THESE DOGS ARE RELAXED AND PLAYFUL, HAVING A GREAT TIME INTERACTING. IT IS SO IMPORTANT FOR DOGS TO HAVE PLAY SESSIONS WITH OTHERS OF THEIR OWN KIND, AS WELL AS PEOPLE. (COURTESY ALI HETHERINGTON)

too. Wolves and dogs hate to be alone, and although many dogs learn to cope with it, they are never truly happy.

Discipline

Discipline should be appropriate, never excessive, and your dog should understood the reason for it. If you leave him on his own for some time and find on your return that he has chewed a book, he will not relate a telling off at this point to what he did probably some while earlier, as that will be long-forgotten. All he will understand is that sometimes when you return you are angry, so may become fearful on each occasion, anxiously trying to read your facial and body expressions and showing appeasing behaviour, just in case.

A good example of this is when I was looking after a friend's dog, with whom I had a great relationship. One day I had a really bad journey home, and was very irritable when I reached the house. The dog would not come anywhere near me, and was making submissive and appeasing gestures. When I eventually worked out why this was, I snapped out of my irritation and she bounded up to me in the usual way. She had done nothing wrong, but was reading the signs I was giving out and reacting to my emotional state. So, if your dog sometimes behaves like this, it could be he's reacting to *your* mood rather than 'feeling guilty' about something.

39

The truth about wolves and dogs

SIMPLY RAISING A TAIL CAN ASSERT AUTHORITY, AND CONTROL
THE BEHAVIOUR OF ANOTHER WOLF ...
(COURTESY PATRICK MELTON)

Scientific proof exists that dogs can 'read' our faces, which give so many clues to what we want, expect or feel. They also can react to the slightest change in our body posture, emotions or thoughts. A wolf I know is so perceptive that even a change in breath rate will tell her something is up, and she will refuse to be caught.

A soft growl or stern word from you is all that most dogs will usually require; there is absolutely no need to shout at, physically strike, or isolate your dog. Keep in mind the qualities of a strong breeding pair – calmness, control and slight aloofness – and the ways in which they administer discipline with a look, or discreet change in body language, which might be as subtle as raising their tail. Strategies I have found useful for wolf discipline are standing my ground, or even walking forward to meet the animal as he jumps up at you, both of which prevent you from appearing vulnerable. I have also placed my hand on the muzzle and gently pushed the head away from me.

A client of mine was being bitten by her young dog as she dragged the

... AS CAN AN INTENT STARE. (COURTESY MONTY SLOAN)

unfortunate animal to 'time out' sessions in the utility room: what should she do, she asked me? I pointed out that I had been with the pair for two hours, managing her dog with subtle body language and soft, spoken commands, not once needing to use time out. I had also not been bitten and the dog was behaving beautifully.

The crux of the matter was that the dog was simply being a dog and getting punished for it. It was young, under-stimulated and untrained, and was being left with the children without adult supervision. During normal play, the children would scream, which would alarm and agitate the pup, especially as the children would then scream every time he approached them, whereupon his owner would decide that he needed to take time out.

In addition to this, the young dog had no toys of his own, was rarely walked, and not shown how to behave properly: he was frustrated, confused and scared, and who can blame him?

Another client had a young puppy that had suddenly become frightened of men. I discovered that someone else in the household (a man) had grabbed the dog to rub her nose in a mess she had made on the floor earlier that evening, and in the process had dropped the dog on her nose. Sometimes, just one incident can create a massive problem, so be very careful with discipline and how you use it; incidentally, this old training method is unnecessarily unkind and, in any case, is not at all effective.

Very often a telling off will only result in your dog not misbehaving whilst you are around, or being afraid of you. Positive reinforcement – giving your dog a reward for doing something that you want him to – is much more effectve in every case.

What makes a good leader/handler?

A good leader:

✔ Never raises their voice, and endeavours to always speak to their dog in their usual tone. It's much more impressive to whisper a command to your dog which he obeys rather than having to holler every time

✔ Is calm in all situations, even if their dog has taken half an hour to recall in the park. Dogs do not understand or equate punishment to something done or not done hours ago: they live in the present. Make good behaviour count by positive reinforcement, and let go what you can't change: the 30 minutes you stood around waiting while your dog was off having so much fun! Ask yourself why your dog prefers being away from you, rather than with you. Are you not interacting with him, and therefore not as interesting as an owner who carries treats in their pocket, and throws toys for their dog?

✔ Assesses every situation and adapts handling accordingly. People often ask how I would deal with this or that situation, but the answer would depend on the situation, my dog's mood, and my own emotional state, so would probably differ each time. Flexibility and adaptablity are key here – plus treating your dog as an individual

✔ Questions what *they*, rather than the dog, are doing wrong, and what needs to change to allow the dog to understand their intention. So, if a lesson is not being learnt, or your dog is not doing what is asked of him, try and think what it is that you can you do to help him understand. Like people, dogs have different learning styles and abilities; days when they are more interested in playing or sleeping, and times when they feel under the weather. When I'm teaching people, I often have to rephrase what I am saying two, sometimes three times before they understand me. I do not get angry with them but just keep changing tack until something resonates with them. Eventually, the light bulb comes on and they will have enjoyed a pleasant, stress-free learning experience. It's the same with your dog. Know when to push, when to change tack, and when to stop and come back to the lesson later

✔ Never uses physical violence. 'Where knowledge ends violence begins' is a good phrase to remember, which will steer you along the right path in potentially stressful situations. In such cases, stop what you are doing and walk away until you and your dog are calm and you can return to the situation. A trick I learnt years ago when things were not going to plan was to laugh. This breaks the mounting tension and, when owners see that you get it wrong sometimes, but that it's no big deal, it gives them the confidence to try themselves.

I've also exclaimed on occasion 'Oh you little darling!' when presented with very challenging canine behaviour, which helps me to remain calm and look at the situation in a different light, when what I really feel might be irritation or frustration.

Reconising these negative thoughts reminds me that it's not usually the dog's fault, and I can then try a different approach whilst remaining calm, or simply stop for a while. Try it – it really works!

✔ Does not use harsh tools and equipment or punishment, both of which, in my opinion, are used by quick-fix trainers, or those who do not understand the cause of the behaviour. Be warned: if this method is used, the unwanted behaviour will always reoccur at a later date. Proper, kind training may take longer initially, but will save hours in the long run, *and* be effective

✔ Is willing to try new methods and change tactics to fit the dog, which goes back to 'where knowledge ends violence begins.' The more tools you have in your metaphorical toolbox the more flexible you can be

✔ Is patient. My approach is if it takes an hour for a dog to feel comfortable with me near him, then it takes an hour. You cannot rush some things, so if you do not have the time, don't become involved. It really doesn't matter if it takes a week to clip your dog's nails, and this is infinitely preferable to putting your dog through a traumatic struggle whilst you try and finish the job in one go

✔ Is willing to address their shortcomings. If you cannot recognise your own shortcomings and limitations, and know how to deal with these, how can you do this with your dog?

✔ Is confident and decisive with their dog when required. Some dogs –

The truth about wolves and dogs

just like some children – may try and take advantage of a situation. You should know when to stand your ground, be the leader, and act in a calm, authoritative way

✔ Uses body language and facial expressions as much as vocal commands to give directions. Dogs are very receptive, and a well-timed look or stare will be much more effective than shouting and waving your arms around

✔ Never subjects a dog to a situation that is too much for them to cope with. Recognise the difference between a little pressure and stress: stress inhibits learning; pressure can enhance it. This is a really important point. If you attend a training class with which your dog is not coping, seek one-to-one training

✔ Recognises a dog's natural instincts and allows him to exhibit natural behaviour in a safe way. Hopefully, you will have researched your dog's breed before taking him home, which will allow you to be imaginative and create ways in which your dog can safely exhibit the natural behaviour bred into him for hundreds, if not thousands of years. Give him a job to do

✔ Is proactive and a good problem-solver. Should your dog behave inappropriately, step in and redirect his attention at an opportune moment.

DOGS NEED PHYSICAL AND MENTAL STIMULATION – AND THE FREEDOM TO BE THEMSELVES. (COURTESY ALI HETHERINGTON)

A change in the management of your dog or the environment may be all that's required to head-off a potential problem

✔ Is respectful to their dog, and will strive to be respected in return, which will have to be earnt

✔ Is flexible: essential for living with and training a dog. Dogs, like wolves, are constantly changing, growing, aging and experiencing life, which is why different training books will give different answers to the same question. New wolf handlers under training complain that every senior handler tells them how to deal with a situation differently: who is right? The answer, of course, is that they ALL are! Each senior handler on each occasion has firstly assessed the mood of the animals, the situation, and the time of year. Wolf behaviour is always more challenging to handlers when hormones are high, for example, and there are other factors to consider, such as what is going on around them, who the handler is, etc. After assessing probably a hundred and one indicators from the wolf, only then will the senior handler choose a course of action that he feels to be right. And this is why a book can never teach you how to be a great dog handler: you have to go out and experience how to do it

Conclusion
The best advice I can give – in the absence of actual experience – is that you listen to everyone, read what you want, and then make an informed judgement about what the training method entails. But also ask yourself two questions: "Does this make sense?" and "Would I be happy for someone to use that method and/or piece of equipment on me?" If the answer to either question is 'no,' you should steer well clear.

Once you become adaptable and consider your dog's emotional, physical and mental states, dog training becomes cooperative and collaborative between the two of you, rather than a battle. Training should not be a case of not allowing your dog to have his way; get this concept right out of your head. You are one half of a partnership, not a commanding general. Once your dog understands that you will listen, support and direct him appropriately, your relationship will blossom. He will begin to listen to every word you say or physical gesture you make, and will take pleasure in doing what you ask, as it is mutually rewarding. So many times I have heard clients whisper to each other: "Look, he's hanging on every word she says," and it's true. Fundamentally, most dogs want to please – but you have to earn the right to that devotion.

Over centuries of association with people, dogs have adapted in every way to please us and fit with our lifestyle. We have changed their body shapes, given and then taken away jobs. We have controlled every aspect of their lives. The modern dog is under more pressure than any generation that came before him. Our lives are so full, and we are so time-poor that we sometimes ignore their wants and needs, which, in turn, can lead to anxiety and frustration, boredom and aggression for our animals.

We tell dogs when they can eat, go to the toilet, play and exercise. You name it, we control it. We've been led to believe that relaxing that control will make our dogs challenge our authority, but, generally dogs want to be what they've always been: our companions, workmates, and a loved and valued part of the family. If you set aside the old rules, let your dog have some choice about how he lives his life, really pay attention to what he is trying to tell you, and then adapt your handling and management of him, your relatiopnship will grow and blossom.

Visit Hubble and Hattie on the web: www.hubblrandhattie.com and www.hubbleandhattie • blogspot.com
twitter • Details of all books • Special offers • Newsletter • New book news

43

Is my dog dominant – or in pain?

As a Tellington TTouch Companion Animal Practitioner, I often come into contact with dogs that have been labelled dominant in nature, as a result of behaviour that has been going on for a long time, or which has suddenly shown itself. As I rarely see true dominance in domestic dogs, I always question owners closely about why they have reached this conclusion.

That hurts!

My interest is particularly roused if, when questioned about their dog's health or any sustained injuries, it transpires that he or she has been knocked over or has run into something, especially if the 'dominant' behaviour became evident after this event. Of course, with a rescue dog it's not always possible to know his history, and he may well have previous or existing health issues, but how many of us automatically assume it is temperament that is the root cause of the aggression, when it could be pain that is causing a dog to act in this manner?

Pain can take many forms as the result of both injury and illness, so can be hard to recognise. Acute pain is easy: your dog steps on something that causes a sharp pain, which then subsides when he removes his paw from that

IT'S RARE TO SEE DOMESTIC DOGS DISPLAYING THE LEVEL OF DOMINANCE SHOWN HERE. (COURTESY OLIVER MATLA)

The truth about wolves and dogs

position. If there's injury as a result, your dog will usually receive veterinary treatment, which will include pain relief if necessary.

However, what if your dog was bowled over while playing with another dog, but, on examination appears to have no injury? Later that day, he growls when you ask him to move, which is completely out of character for him. Do you assume your dog is being 'dominant' or do you consider whether he may have been injured by the incident earlier in the day? How about if your dog is quiet for a few days after receiving a knock but appears to pick up, then, months later, growls at you or is hesitant about jumping into the car as usual? What would you assume then? If my dog normally had a sweet nature and loved the car, my first thought would always be: is he in pain?

Young puppies can receive injuries which go undetected; for example, if they roll out of the bed when playing with their littermates, and damage their neck. Once placed in a home, this small bundle of fluff may growl at the children when they are playing with him, whereupon he is labelled bad-tempered and of a dominant nature. Seeking advice on how to deal with the issue often results in mismanagement of the situation, and your puppy being subjected to harsh training methods, which are at best inappropriate and at worst highly damaging to your relationship. It also means that his pain has gone undiagnosed and he is still suffering, but by now he may have decided that he cannot express himself in a natural way to let you know that he is hurting. If this is the case, in time he may become depressed and withdrawn, or reluctant to be touched. This sort of behaviour may even escalate into aggressive outbursts.

As dogs get older, arthritic changes occur, and other pain-related conditions can develop. Many times I have asked owners whether their dog is on pain relief for arthritis because he appears stiff, only to be told that he 'doesn't need it.' Yet their dog is obviously feeling some level of discomfort, which they seem unable or unwilling to recognise.

A small dog I saw years ago was a classic example. I was called in because the dog was rushing at people, barking and growling as they walked past him in the house. As I watched him, I noticed he would hold up one hind leg when doing this. On investigation, it transpired that the little dog had arthritis, but was not receiving any pain relief, and the vibration that resulted from people walking across the wooden floor was causing him discomfort. Once on appropriate medication, this behaviour ceased.

Undiagnosed pain and discomfort can also dent a dog's confidence, and this is often the case with show dogs, who may back away from the judge, growl on examination, and/or refuse to enter the ring.

One dog I worked with lost her confidence a few months before Crufts, the well-known dog show held annually in Birmingham, England. After several sessions of Tellington TTouch she had improved slightly, but when I felt her back I found four prominent hotspots along her spine that remained whichever TTouches I used. Although she moved beautifully with no sign of lameness or pain, I asked her owner to take her to a McTimoney Chiropractor who was qualified to work with animals. On examination her spine was found to be out of alignment in every single hotspot I had located. Once treated, Tellington TTouch sorted the rest and the dog came tenth in her group that year at Crufts.

Her owner has learned to spot the signs of discomfort and her dog receives regular checks. Result: one happy dog.

Pain symptoms are not always as obvious as limping or whimpering, and may show as a subtle change in body posture or facial expression. Your dog might stop grooming himself, or begin to self-harm; he may sleep more or hide under beds; lose his appetite, and/or enthusiasm for walks. He may become protective of a particular area of his body or limbs, or react aggressively if touched there; still others become restless and demanding. Even the quality and rate of the breath can help you to detect a problem, for example, if a dog is shallow-breathing, which means that normal ribcage expansion is not seen. If your dog begins acting out of character, pay close attention in order to understand what is happening with him.

If help is required, your first port of call should be your vet, of course, although it is sometimes difficult to diagnose a problem from an examination alone, and further tests or a referral to an orthopaedic surgeon or canine physiotherapist may be necessary.

An eight-month-old Belgian Shepherd called Billy came to a Tellington TTouch workshop I was taking. He occasionally limped: it was very slight but his owner was concerned. When I later worked with the dog in a one-to-one session, we noticed that he stumbled often, and was placing less weight on his left foreleg. He frequently held up that paw, and was anxious when we touched the leg. I talked to the dog's owner about getting him assessed by the canine physiotherapist at Greyfriars Rehabilitation and Hydrotherapy Referral Centre, near Guildford. Billy's owner later wrote to update me:

"I sorted out a referral to Greyfriars for Billy to see the physio and for some hydrotherapy sessions. The physio found a problem with Billy's left elbow. Things seemed to be settling down, but just over a fortnight ago Billy went lame again after running around the garden. I spoke to Greyfriars and they agreed that I should get a referral for Billy to see a specialist. I went back to my vet who referred me on. Billy had X-rays and the outcome was that he had elbow dysplasia in the left foreleg. He had keyhole surgery to correct the problem, and this was a complete success."

Under careful management Billy now leads a full and pain-free life. As the condition was spotted relatively early, wear and tear on the joint can be managed and minimised. A great outcome, and all down to the owner's determination to help her dog.

A key thing to remember is that, as a survival tactic, dogs will endeavour to hide pain and cope with varying degrees of discomfort apparently well. All dogs have different pain thresholds: Greyhound owners will tell you that their dog will scream at the slightest knock, whereas bull breeds could have a leg hanging off, but will appear indifferent. I always try to imagine it from the dog's perspective. Some dogs need regular maintenance sessions with a qualified canine osteopath or chiropractor, just as some people do. Your dog may suffer pain only when carrying out a certain activity, after hard exercise, or in damp weather. He may have come to carry himself in such a way that alleviates the pain he is feeling, but should you ask him to stand in a particular way, or actually move him physically, the pain could suddenly catch him, causing a reaction that can easily be misinterpreted.

So many behaviours come about because of discomfort, and we must appreciate that the pain and discomfort our dogs feel as a result of injury or illness is just as real and just as horrid as the pain we feel. We should not let a genetic predisposition to hide an injury result in our canine companions being misunderstood by those they trust the most.

What to do if you suspect your dog is in pain

A change in character or behaviour is often the first sign that your dog is in pain. How your dog moves is also an important indicator: how is he holding himself when he walks? If you imitate that movement, how does it feel, and what other parts of your body begin to suffer with referred pain as a result? It's amazing how many times a light bulb has come on in my head when I do this exercise. For example, if you turn out your wrists to imitate a dog that walks on the outside of his forefeet you can feel tension building in what would be the outside of a dog's lower foreleg and shoulders.

If you suspect your dog of having an injury or condition that is causing him pain or discomfort, but it is intermittent, or your vet cannot diagnose a problem, be persistent: you know your dog the best, so trust your instinct. Sometimes it's the case that what appears to be the obvious cause of pain or discomfort is not actually the main problem; for example, many dogs with foreleg lameness actually have a problem in the neck. If necessary, seek a second opinion or a referral, either to a specialist vet or a centre like Greyfriars which can assess your dog in multiple ways. Or ask your vet to prescribe a course of painkillers to see if this makes a difference. Pain is much better understood by vets these days, as student training in this area is far more advanced. The range of drugs is also improving.

I was asked for my opinion about a friend's elderly dog, who had suddenly become very clingy, and did not appear to like any of the minders her owner left her with when out of the house. My first suggestion was to check her pain relief and, when that was increased, the behaviour stopped.

Whatever modality of treatment you choose – be it osteopathy, physiotherapy, chiropractic, homeopathic or traditional medicine – all can shed light on physical problems, and using several together can be even more effective.

I often see dogs whose owners know they're not 'right,' but the vet has not been able to identify why. A Tellington TTouch Practitioner or physiotherapist, for example, may be able to identify more clearly what is going on because the dog will be in a much less stressful environment, where time constraints are not so much of an issue. As a result, the dog should be less concerned with trying to conceal the problem: we often find that TTouch treatment will enable other practitioners to achieve more as the animal's body is better prepared. For example, it will help the animal begin to release any tension, and also provide some pain relief. In addition, it will promote the release of feel-good endorphins such as serotonin and dopamine. The dog will benefit for longer from work by other practitioners, such as chiropractors, as posture

is also improved. If treatments are done in isolation it can mean the body reverts to its old, out-of-alignment posture.

Alba, a wolf I helped rehabilitate after a spinal injury, needed a TTouch session before his physiotherapy exercises because, otherwise, he would air-snap and guard his body, and we would achieve a far smaller range of movement with his physio exercises. TTouch is also great for pain relief and assisting mobility, and sits really well with veterinary and other complementary care, be this traditional or alternative.

Don't be afraid to be proactive and try a range of methods, though be sure to do your research, and establish that the person who will be working with your dog is qualified to do so. Also seek your vet's advice in this respect, and note that any good practitioner will insist on your vet's permission before working on your animal.

MAI AT UKWCT. (COURTESY LEE PIPER)

47

HOW TO
UNDERSTAND
YOUR DOG

Dogs communicate using all of their senses: sight, sound, scent, touch. But although many of us live with dogs on a daily basis, we often miss all but the most obvious of their signals.

Claims that a dog has bitten for no reason, without warning, are rarely accurate; it's much more likely to be the case that the first two or three levels of communication the dog has attempted have been missed. Dogs can be incredibly subtle with their signals, or, like us, not express their feelings very clearly. Others, due to their breed or temperament, may move more quickly through the levels of communication, making it difficult for us to recognise and appreciate all of the signs. Before you know it, the dog has to 'shout' at us – escalate his behaviour – in order to be understood.

In this chapter we will look at the main areas of canine body language, which should make it easier for you to recognise and read the signals that your dog is giving you. Don't worry; it's much easier than learning a foreign language, and you can become fluent in 'dog-speak' very easily. An important point to remember is that a single action can have more than one meaning, which is why it's essential to read the whole body, and take into account the circumstances and situation in order to arrive at the correct interpretation.

For example, a tongue flick or lick of the nose can be simply removing food from the nose, a way of enhancing a smell, a sign of anxiety or nervousness, or, in the case of a rapid tongue flick, the precursor to a bite.

Wherever possible, photos are supplied to demonstrate the points made.

Calming signals

The first level of communication – often missed – are calming signals. Think of them as whispers: your dog is discreetly letting you know that he is anxious about a situation. If you can spot these signs you can really help your dog through many difficult scenarios.

Calming signals were first noted in wolf packs, and in the wolf world are known as 'cut-off signals.' A lot of what we call 'ritualised aggression' occurs within the pack, and what appear to be highly aggressive exchanges are mostly only noise and show. It was noted by biologists that if aggression toward a lower ranking animal was high, this animal displayed certain signals in an effort to interrupt or 'cut' the level of aggression, ultimately calming the situation.

A few decades ago a Norwegian called Turid Rugaas further developed this area of study with wolves when she noticed domestic dogs presenting the same signals. By understanding and even using the gestures ourselves,

MAI, LYING ON THE GROUND, ANXIOUSLY LICKS HER NOSE AS THE PLAY SESSION BEGINS TO GET A LITTLE OVERWHELMING. SHE IS FEELING THREATENED, AND HAS ASKED THE OTHERS TO BACK OFF WITH THIS CUT-OFF SIGNAL (KNOWN AS A CALMING SIGNAL IN DOGS). (COURTESY PATRICK MELTON)

MOSI IS CLEARLY NOT LICKING HER NOSE TO REMOVE FOOD. NOTE THE SET OF THE EARS, THE INTENT GAZE. AND TENSION IN HER MUZZLE. HER SHOULDERS ARE ALSO HUNCHED, READY FOR ACTION. (COURTESY OLIVER MATLA)

IF YOUR DOG BEGINS TO SNIFF AS ANOTHER DOG APPROACHES, THEY MAY BE HAVING A DIALOGUE. WATCH BOTH DOGS CLOSELY, AND NOTE THE SIGNALS GOING BACK AND FORTH BETWEEN THE TWO. (COURTESY EMMA COLEMAN, BLINK PHOTOGRAPHY)

OF COURSE, IT COULD EQUALLY BE SIMPLY AN INTERESTING SMELL: LOOK AT THE WHOLE SITUATION AND ENVIRONMENT BEFORE DECIDING WHAT'S GOING ON. (COURTESY OLIVER MATLA)

we can comprehend the very first whispers of canine communication. If correctly interpreted, this may even prevent a situation getting to a defensive/ aggressive stage, and allow us to help a dog through a scary situation by keeping him calmer. If we also use the same signals in response, this can really help establish a rapport, deepening the relationship and building trust between our two species.

From our perspective, by learning to recognise and correctly interpret calming signals we will become much more intuitive handlers. For example, when working with a nervous dog, I always yawn and look away, or 'slow eye blink' at him; before long, he responds in kind and often begins to approach and interact wth me.

The best place to observe calming signals is on a walk. Observe your dog as he spots another dog coming toward him. If both have good communication skills they will begin a dialogue the second they see each other, even from a

MOSI'S TONGUE FLICK – WHICH IS STRAIGHT AND FLICKING RAPIDLY – IS CLEARLY WARNING OTHER WOLVES TO KEEP AWAY FROM HER FOOD. THIS SIGNAL CAN BE USED FOR MANY REASONS, INCLUDING DISTANCING BEHAVIOUR, THREAT OF ATTACK, APPEASEMENT, ETC. THE CLUE TO MOSI'S INTENT IS HER POSTURE. SHE IS DISPLAYING AEROPLANE EARS (TURNED TO THE SIDE AND FACING DOWN), A LOWERED HEAD, AND 'HARD' (INTENT) EYES. HER LIPS ARE FORWARD AND SHE HAS BUNCHED HER MUSCLES AND HALF LIFTED HER LEFT LEG IN PREPARATION OF A LUNGE OR RETREAT WITH HER PRIZE.
(COURTESY PATRICK MELTON)

MAPLE IS CLEARLY WARY OF SOMETHING IN THIS PHOTO: HER TONGUE IS CURLED UP OVER THE NOSE; EARS ARE TIGHT AND UP, AND HER FACE SHOWS SIGNS OF TENSION, INCLUDING A SLIGHTLY FURROWED FOREHEAD AND RAISED EYEBROWS. MAPLE'S EYES ARE NARROWED AND ALSO SLIGHTLY GLAZED. NOSE LICKING AND TONGUE FLICKS CAN MEAN MANY THINGS, BUT GENERALLY INDICATE AROUSAL OF SOME KIND, WHICH COULD BE GOOD OR BAD. THE WAY TO DECIDE WHICH IS AFFECTING YOUR DOG IS TO READ HER ENTIRE BODY LANGUAGE IN ORDER TO ASSESS THE SITUATION. MAPLE IS ANXIOUS ABOUT SOMETHING, AND THE NOSE LICK SHOWS SHE IS TRYING TO CALM THE SITUATION.
(COURTESY EMMA COLEMAN, BLINK PHOTOGRAPHY)

distance. Every dog has favourite signals, but will often use a vast repertoire when the situation requires it.

The meeting may involve any of the following scenarios: one of the dogs may reduce speed whilst the other sniffs the ground, precluding the possibility of a direct stare; the other may turn his head, or flick his tongue across his nose, scenting the air, or slowly blink. One dog may urinate to show a lack of intent or threat, and either animal may sit down with their back to the other.

51

The truth about wolves and dogs

IT'S VERY CLEAR WHAT THIS FEMALE IS FEELING. HER LIPS ARE FORWARD, THE TONGUE IS RIDGED AND CURLED, AND THE EYE IS HARD. SHE HAS AN AGONISTIC PUCKER (PUCKERING OF THE WHISKER AREA), AS WELL AS A LUMPY WHISKER BED (BUMPS ON HER MUZZLE WHERE THE WHISKERS ARE STANDING UP AND FORWARD), AND HER HACKLES ARE UP. SHE IS OBVIOUSLY NOT IN THE MOOD FOR MATING. NOTICE HOW DIFFERENT THESE LAST TWO PHOTOS ARE FROM MAPLE ANXIOUSLY LICKING HER NOSE (PREVIOUS PAGE). DOGS RARELY GET TO THE LEVEL OF AROUSAL SHOWN HERE WHERE THEY TONGUE FLICK TO INDICATE THEIR INTENTION TO ATTACK, BUT IT IS SOMETIMES SEEN. (COURTESY OLIVER MATLA)

HUMPHREY IS CONCERNED ABOUT HAVING HIS FOOT PICKED UP, AS INDICATED BY HIS SLOW EYE BLINK. (COURTESY VICKY ALHADEFF)

If the approaching dog lacks communication skills, your dog may escalate his behaviour as the other approaches, because if his polite signals which ask if the other dog is a threat are ignored, he has no way of knowing what might happen when they meet face-to-face. In this situation, your dog may use bolder body language, or vocalisation to 'shout' a little louder, which, in the worst case, could result in a full-blown fight if not carefully handled by the dogs' owners.

In my experience, those dogs which are aggressive toward others usually are out of fear (this relates to the 'fight/fear' response which I discuss later). Most of the 'fear-aggressive' dogs I have worked with will show calming signals at first sight of another dog. If the situation is handled correctly the signals gradually diminish, but may increase to barking, growling, lunging,

THIS LITTLE DOG IS TRYING TO CALM A VERY STRESSFUL SITUATION. YOU CAN TELL SHE IS UNDER PRESSURE AS HER WHOLE BODY IS TIGHT AND HER FOOT IS LIFTED, AND NOTE THE TENSION IN HER SHOULDER, JAW, FOREHEAD AND EARS. THE EYE HAS A WORRIED CAST AND THE LIPS ARE BEGINNING TO COME FORWARD, INDICATING SHE IS ALMOST READY TO MOVE FROM A CALMING SIGNAL TO ATTACK IF THE SITUATION DOES NOT ABATE SOON. (PHOTO BY EMMA COLEMAN, BLINK PHOTOGRAPHY, TAKEN COURTESY OF WALKABOUT DOG TRAINING GROUP)

AS THE TWO DOGS ON THE RIGHT OF THIS PHOTO FACE OFF, THE DOG ON THE LEFT IS DELIBERATELY STAYING NEUTRAL AND TRYING TO CALM THE SITUATION BY WALKING BETWEEN THE TWO AND SPLITTING THEM. (PHOTO BY LEE PIPER, TAKEN COURTESY OF WALKABOUT DOG TRAINING GROUP)

The truth about wolves and dogs

ARCHIE AND ANGEL ARE USING JAW FENCING AS PART OF THEIR PLAY SESSION. NOTE THE NEUTRAL BODY LANGUAGE AND 'SOFT' EYES, INDICATING THAT, ALTHOUGH THIS IS A FORM OF RITUALISED AGGRESSION (THE MOVEMENTS AND POSTURES ARE EXAGGERATED; WHAT ARE KNOWN AS META-SIGNALS), IT'S MEANT IN FUN. (COURTESY KAREN BUSH)

etc, all the way to a bite in some cases if not. Most of the time even this is ritualised, and not liable to do too much harm, although some dogs will bite hard and cause damage if they perceive a threat.

In wolves and dogs ritualised aggression is noisy and dramatic – the forelegs come off the ground and the lips are drawn back, indicating that this is a pseudo attack. A full-on fight is less noisy and more purposeful; all four legs stay on the ground and the lips come forward.

Once you have watched and understood how your dog interacts with other dogs, you will be able to note if and when he directs calming signals at people and/or objects. These can be quite noticeable when you are carrying out what your dog may consider to be an 'invasive' activity such as grooming, nail clipping, bathing, etc, at which times, even the serenest of canines – who appear to be comfortable with what you're doing – can exhibit a calming signal. Sometimes, even noises or objects will elicit the same response. Occasionally, some dogs are not as skilful at handling a situation, and will quickly run through their repetoire of calming signals, and then threatening behaviour until the point of no return. Such animals need very careful handling as they lack the ability to let you know what they are feeling. This is often the case with a rescue dog, which may have come from very difficult circumstances, and with dogs who have been isolated from other canines from a very young age, and have therefore never developed these communication skills.

Should you notice your dog giving a signal, stop and consider the situation. Dogs frequently give calming signals – these are part of the way they communicate, after all – but if what you are doing could be the reason for his signals, consider your approach. Is it, maybe, that you are feeling cross or upset? Are you standing over your dog in a dominant way? Have you inadvertently invaded his space to the extent that he feels cornered?

As primates, we can accept and, indeed, seek physical contact a lot more than do canines. We constantly over-handle our dogs; touching, patting, moving them many times during a day, and possibly suddenly and without warning. Sometimes, all that is necessary is to allow them time to notice and understand what we are about to do: a few minutes' TTouch bodywork, or simply yawning and looking away may reassure your dog that he need not feel threatened. Many times I have 'talked' (used canine calming signals) with a nervous dog for a while before he or she feels it is safe to approach me. Or I have been able to touch a dog in a certain area of his body because we have communicated via calming signals: by signalling back we acknowledge their concern and present no threat. You'll find that often dogs will seem relieved and in awe of you once they can see you understand them.

THIS DOG IS DISPLAYING A HIGH LEVEL OF TENSION THAT COULD TIP OVER INTO AGGRESSION IF ANOTHER DOG OR PERSON COMES NEAR. HER LIPS ARE FORWARD AND HER FACE APPEARS 'WOODEN,' AND SHE HAS THE BEGINNINGS OF PUCKERING OF THE WHISKER AREA (AGONISTIC PUCKER). THIS DOG'S ATTACK – IF IT COMES – WILL BE SILENT. (PHOTO BY EMMA COLEMAN, BLINK PHOTOGRAPHY, TAKEN COURTESY OF WALKABOUT DOG TRAINING GROUP)

IN THIS SHOT THE DOG ON THE RIGHT IS CLEARLY DISPLAYING TWO CALMING SIGNALS: YAWNING AND AVERTING HER GAZE FROM THE OTHER TWO. THE DIRECT LOOK OF THE COLLIE IN THE MIDDLE IS A LITTLE FULL-ON. BOTH OF THE DOGS ON THE LEFT HAVE THEIR TAILS SLIGHTLY RAISED TO INDICATE INTEREST, IN DIRECT CONTRAST TO THE DOG ON THE RIGHT WHO HAS A TUCKED TAIL AND FURLED EARS: THUS ANOTHER INDICATION THAT SHE IS FEELING ANXIOUS. (COURTESY SARAH HARRIS)

IN A DIFFERENT SITUATION, WHEN THE YAWN AND EYE AVERT SIGNALS DO NOT APPEAR TO CALM THE SITUATION, SHE LIES DOWN. NOTE HER FURLED EARS, TIGHT FOREHEAD, EYE AVERT, AND SLIGHT LIFT OF THE RIGHT FORELEG. SHE MAY BE LYING DOWN BUT SHE'S CERTAINLY NOT RELAXED: EVERY PART OF HER BODY IS SET TO RESPOND IF NECESSARY. (COURTESY SARAH HARRIS)

The easiest calming signal for us to give is to yawn and look away from our dog, but avoid just standing there completely still, as dogs stand rigid as a fear response, or sometimes just prior to attack. Relax and 'soften' your body to make yourself appear smaller and breathe slowly. Turn your body slightly so that you are not directly facing your dog, and avoid direct eye contact as this can be perceived as threatening.

A dog that came on one of my workshops was nervous of people. As the owner was signing in, I approached the pair, but sat down on a step near the dog. Side-on to the animal. I did not look at her but spoke softly to her owner, whilst giving calming signals, such as yawning and slow blinking, to let the dog know that I was not a threat. Within a minute the dog had approached and invited me to interact with her; we became friends straight away.

A little while later I was still sitting on the step fussing her when someone new entered the room. The dog began to bark. The new person stood still and very upright; the barking increased. I was looking at the situation from the dog's point of view – both mentally and physically as I was at her level – and even I felt threatened by this body posture, so quickly asked the individual to simply walk away, which resolved the issue. If you consider the situation from the point of view of a dog, you will realise that being stared at, or approached by someone with hands held out in front of them, who is also talking loudly, and showing lots of teeth as they do so, can appear very threatening indeed.

All animals, including humans, give calming signals, sometimes without realising. Learn to read these signals and you will enjoy a rare insight into your dog's world.

Fear responses – the five Fs

There are at least five known fear responses that animals and people will display, and the two best known are flight and fight: run away or stand and fight. Which of these two responses is chosen has to do with many things, but is also instinctive, and to change this requires conscious thought and effort. Two individuals in the same threatening situation may react differently, and it's the same for dogs.

When I worked for Guide Dogs for the Blind as a live-in kennel staff member back in the 1980s, we would respond to student alarms, never knowing what to expect until we got to the room. As many clients were diabetic, it could be a life-threatening situation, so my response to an alarm was to run at top speed toward the room, adrenaline flowing. It was the same with fire alarm drills – I had to run, even though I knew there was no danger. I loved that jolt of adrenaline, the expectation that something exciting, if scary, was happening. Maybe I'm an adrenaline-junkie, but that's how I instinctively react. But everyone is different, and this is why dogs react differently to the same situation or a perceived threat, due in part to their make-up, temperament and, I suspect, previous experiences.

So, fight and flight are self-explanatory. But what about the fear response 'fool around,' or, as it is sometimes known 'fidget about'? When our dogs seem to be acting the fool, we may automatically assume they are playing, having a bit of fun, but maybe we should look at the situation and assess their fear level? 'Fool around,' as a strategy, works for the dog. Consider if you are trying to groom your dog, and he starts acting up, making you laugh.

This dog is displaying at least six body and facial expressions that convey how she feels. Can you spot them? The obvious ones are her tucked tail and tight, furled ears, but she is also blinking, and her muzzle is beginning to show a lumpy whisker bed. The paw lift indicates she is unsure of the situation, and can be a prelude to aggressive behaviour. In this case, the dog is showing signs of fear ...

... and went on to display classic signs of the fear/fight response. Her ears are furled and lips are held in a wide 'C' shape with puckered, lumpy whisker bed. She is showing whale eye (whites of the eye). The dog on the right is also showing whale eye but in this case it's because he's looking to the right at the dog who is attacking him. (Photo by Emma Coleman Blink Photography, taken courtesy of Walkabout Dog Training Group)

Mosi, the wolf being chased, is under pressure, and not enjoying the game: note the aeroplane ears, arched back, and full tongue extension, plus her furrowed brow and hooded look to her eye. Mai, the black wolf directly behind Mosi, is in a heightened state of play which could easily flip to an aggressive attack. Torak, the lighter-coloured wolf, is obviously simply enjoying the game. Mosi, the wolf being chased, is in flight mode. (Courtesy Patrick Melton)

DOGS WILL START OFF WITH A CALMING SIGNAL, SHOW FEAR IN THEIR BODY LANGUAGE, AND THEN ESCALATE INTO A FEAR RESPONSE IF NOT LISTENED TO. THIS LITTLE DOG, EXTREMELY ANXIOUS ABOUT THE SITUATION, WAS FLIPPING BETWEEN CALMING SIGNALS, FIGHT AND FREEZE, TRYING TO GET THE OTHER DOG TO LISTEN TO HER. (PHOTO BY EMMA COLEMAN BLINK PHOTOGRAPHY, TAKEN COURTESY OF WALKABOUT DOG TRAINING GROUP)

ground in a dead-faint. This is rare, but do consider that this is what might have happened if the situation may have warranted an extreme reaction.

Whichever fear response a dog uses, it's probable that it will be at least the third or fourth indicator you will get that all is not well. Physical changes that can occur post calming signals are glazed eyes, red sclera (the white part of the eye), showing the whites of the eye or even bulging eyes. It's often possible to note a change in your dog's breathing rate, swiftly followed by a fear response. If you know what to look for, you can help prevent your dog from progressing past this stage, or at least recognise it as it happens. Be aware that stress inhibits learning, so if your dog is showing a fear response in a training situation, you may as well stop and go home, because he will not be open and responsive to learning in this state, and attempts to continue training him may well exacerbate the situaiton.

Body language

Much has been written about canine body language. Posture can tell you so much about how a dog is feeling, but when reading body language, it's important to look at the body as a whole to get the full picture. A wagging tail is often misinterpreted: a slow, low wag can be a threatening gesture, just as a fast, stiff wag can denote anxiety. If you own a dog it's really important that you take the time to understand this vital form of dog communication, which – like calming signals and vocalisation – is fundamental to the success of your relationship.

To really understand body language read Barbara Handelman's *Canine Behaviour, A Photo Illustrated Handbook*. I have not come across a better book to understanding your dog's behaviour and body language. In the meantime, the following photo section provides an overview of facial, expressions, body language, and dominant and submissive postures.

Facial expressions

Dogs' expressions can tell you so much of what you need to know to read their emotions and intent. They can portray curiosity, sadness, confusion, and fear, to name just a few.

Body speak

Canine body language is complex, subtle and sophisticated, and can be easily missed if you don't know what to look for. Being able to read the body language of a dog that is approaching, when on a walk, say, can help you to decide if it is safe and apropriate for your dog to interact with him.

You might stop the grooming, laugh, and join in his game. Result? Your dog has cleverly manipulated you into stopping the activity he finds scary or uncomfortable, and diverted you to a less threatening activity. Even if you become annoyed at him and give up, his 'fool around' fear response has achieved the result he wanted.

You can see human examples of the fool around tactic at parties, and in the school playground. Those individuals who make others laugh with words or actions are often the ones lacking in confidence. It obviates the need for a normal interaction with others, and diverts attention from their lack of social skills. Dogs use this ploy a lot, and it is the most misunderstood and ignored fear response of the five. Next time you see your dog act in this way, stop and consider the situation. What is he reacting to? If it's you, modify your activity until he becomes calmer. If it's something in the environment or vicinity, do what you can to remove him from the situation. Use calming signals to help him settle down.

Although dogs often have a favourite fear response which they routinely use, they can sometimes switch between signals, or run through the entire range. If the first signal doesn't seem to work, they may try another, then another if still no response. Each dog differs in the order that signals are tried, but I find one of the hardest to deal with is the freeze, where the dog goes very still, to the extent that even their eyes glaze over and look 'dead.' In my experience, freezing can be very dangerous because a dog in this state can often flip from freeze to fight and, before you know it, you have been bitten by a dog that seconds before was as still as a statue.

Very occasionally, the fifth response – 'faint' – occurs, which is where an animal is literally so terrified that his body shuts down and he drops to the

continued page 65

The truth about wolves and dogs

THE DOG ON THE LEFT IS BEING ASSESSED BY WALKABOUT DOG TRAINING FOR HIS BEHAVIOUR TOWARD OTHER DOGS. THEY ARE WORKING IN A CONTROLLED ENVIRONMENT WITH STOOGE DOGS (USED TO TEACH CANINES WITH BEHAVIOURAL PROBLEMS), AND HE IS WEARING A LONG LINE IN CASE THE TRAINERS NEED TO STEP IN. THE DOG BEING ASSESSED IS SHOWING FEAR AGGRESSION: HIS HACKLES ARE UP AND HIS TAIL – THOUGH RAISED – IS NOT IN THE HIGH POSITION THAT WOULD INDICATE A DOMINANT PERSONALITY. HIS FACE IS SHOWING NUMEROUS SIGNS OF STRESS, INCLUDING A WHALE EYE, AEROPLANE EARS, AND FURROWED BROW. HIS POSTURE IS LOW, INDICATING HE IS UNSURE OF THE SITUATION. (PHOTO BY EMMA COLEMAN BLINK PHOTOGRAPHY, TAKEN COURTESY OF WALKABOUT DOG TRAINING GROUP)

THE FEARFUL DOG IS NOW ON THE RIGHT: HIS TAIL IS TUCKED UNDER, AND HIS WEIGHT IS BACK, INDICATING AN OFFENSIVE POSTURE. THE STOOGE DOG IS REMAINING FAIRLY NEUTRAL, THOUGH IS NOT BACKING DOWN. (PHOTO BY LEE PIPER, TAKEN COURTESY OF WALKABOUT DOG TRAINING GROUP)

EVENTUALLY, THE FEARFUL DOG GOES TO ATTACK THE STOOGE, WHO REACTS. IN BOTH DOGS THE LIPS ARE NOT DRAWN FORWARD AND THE MOUTH IS GAPING. THE STOOGE DOG IS PRIMARILY USING HIS FOOT TO PUSH THE OTHER DOG AWAY IN A FOOT STAB. THIS INTERACTION WAS MOSTLY NOISE, ALTHOUGH THE STOOGE (WHO BARELY RAISED HIS HACKLES) DID HAVE TO MUZZLE NIP THE OTHER ANIMAL TO CONTROL THE SITUATION. (PHOTO BY LEE PIPER, TAKEN COURTESY OF WALKABOUT DOG TRAINING GROUP)

THE OTHER STOOGE DOG TRIES TO COME BETWEEN THE TWO TO CALM THE SITUATION. BEING FEMALE SHE MAY SEEM LESS OF A THREAT TO THE FEARFUL DOG BUT, OUT OF ALL OF THEM, IT IS SHE WHO HAS RAISED HER TAIL, THOUGH REMAINING VERY 'SOFT' AND NEUTRAL IN HER FACIAL EXPRESSIONS. (PHOTO BY LEE PIPER, TAKEN COURTESY OF WALKABOUT DOG TRAINING GROUP)

SHE REMAINED CALM THROUGHOUT THE ENTIRE ALTERCATION. ALTHOUGH THE FEARFUL DOG IS SHOWING SIGNS OF STRESS IN HIS BODY LANGUAGE AND FACIAL FEATURES, SHE DID HELP SIGNIFICANTLY TO SOOTHE HIM WITH HER CALM, NEUTRAL, SUPPORTIVE APPROACH. OF COURSE, THIS METHOD OF TRAINING SHOULD ONLY EVER BY USED BY COMPETENT HANDLERS, AND WILL NOT BE SUITABLE FOR ALL DOGS, IN ANY CASE. (PHOTO BY LEE PIPER, TAKEN COURTESY OF WALKABOUT DOG TRAINING GROUP)

CONSIDER THE WHOLE PICTURE HERE. THE DOG ON THE LEFT – WHO WE HAVE PREVIOUSLY SEEN INTERACTING WITH A LARGER DOG – IS MUCH MORE COMFORTABLE WITH THE WESTIE. SHE'S STILL DISPLAYING SOME CALMING SIGNALS, BUT HER FACE AND EYE ARE MUCH SOFTER. DESPITE SHOWING SIGNS OF CONCERN, THIS INTERACTION ENDED WELL. (PHOTO BY EMMA COLEMAN, BLINK PHOTOGRAPHY, TAKEN COURTESY OF WALKABOUT DOG TRAINING GROUP)

The truth about wolves and dogs

LEFT: INITIAL IMPRESSIONS SUGGEST THAT THIS DOG IS CONFIDENT AND RELAXED, BUT ALERT. HOWEVER, NOTICE THE SLIGHTLY ARCHED BACK; LIKE A COILED SPRING. HIS FACE WEARS A VERY WORRIED EXPRESSION, AND THE FOOT BEING LIFTED IN EXAGGERATED FASHION AND LOWERED HEAD INDICATE THAT ALL IS NOT WELL. (PHOTO BY EMMA COLEMAN, BLINK PHOTOGRAPHY, TAKEN COURTESY OF WALKABOUT DOG TRAINING GROUP)

DAKOTA IS SHOWING THE FIRST SIGN OF A WORRIED EXPRESSION AS SHE WATCHES FOR OTHER WOLVES WHO MIGHT TAKE HER TREAT. NOTE THE RAISED EYEBROWS AND EARS HELD IN A BACKWARD POSITION. (COURTESY PATRICK MELTON)

THE BLACK DOG IN THE FOREGROUND IS SHOWING WHALE EYE, WHICH IS MOST OFTEN SEEN WHEN DOGS FEEL THREATENED OR STRESSED. HIS FACE IS ALSO SHOWING TENSION, MAKING IT SEEM AS IF HE IS SUCKING IN HIS CHEEKS. THE EARS OF THIS DOG ARE PINCHED – AGAIN, A SIGN OF FEAR OR STRESS. COMPARE THIS DOG'S FACE TO THAT OF THE DOG IN THE BACKGROUND WHICH IS RELAXED AND CALM.
(COURTESY ALI HETHERINGTON)

THE GERMAN SHEPHERD IS DISPLAYING 'SEAL EARS:' THEY ARE TIGHTLY FURLED AND HELD FAR BACK ON THE HEAD, WHICH INDICATES FEAR OR APPEASEMENT BEHAVIOUR. THE WORRIED LOOK IN THE DILATED EYES AND TENSION ACROSS THE FOREHEAD CONFIRM THAT HE IS CONCERNED ABOUT THE SITUATION, OR WHAT IS AROUND HIM. (PHOTO BY EMMA COLEMAN, BLINK PHOTOGRAPHY, TAKEN COURTESY OF WALKABOUT DOG TRAINING GROUP)

IN CONTRAST THIS DOG IS ALERT BUT RELAXED, WITH A HIGH EAR CARRIAGE AND SOFT EYES. (PHOTO BY EMMA COLEMAN, BLINK PHOTOGRAPHY, TAKEN COURTESY OF WALKABOUT DOG TRAINING GROUP)

A LEVEL OF REACTION RARELY SEEN IN DOMESTIC DOGS, THIS WOLF IS SHOWING CLASSIC SIGNS OF FEAR AGGRESSION. THE AEROPLANE EARS, (WHICH IS SEEN IN DOGS) SHOW THAT THE WOLF HAS CONFLICTING EMOTIONS: HIS HEAD IS LOW IN DEFENSIVE MODE, COMPLETE WITH LUMPY WHISKER BED AND AGONISTIC PUCKER. HIS BODY LANGAUGE – AND ESPECIALLY HIS TAIL – SHOW HE IS FEELING EXTREMELY THREATENED. HE IS NOT A CONFIDENT, HIGH-RANKING ANIMAL. (COURTESY OLIVER MATLA)

61

The truth about wolves and dogs

LIKE DOGS, WOLVES WILL ALSO TUCK THEIR HINDQUARTERS RIGHT UNDER, GIVING THEM A HUNCHED APPEARANCE, AND CAN EVEN RUN IN THIS POSTURE. THE FACE CLEARLY SAYS 'STAY AWAY' BUT THE EARS, TAIL AND BODY TELL US HE IS FEELING THREATENED, AND IS ALSO FEARFUL. (COURTESY OLIVER MATLA)

BOTH OF THESE DOGS ARE ALERT, BUT THE DOG ON THE RIGHT-HAND SIDE IS ALSO CONCERNED. HE HAS TUCKED IN HIS CHIN, IS SHOWING SLIGHT WHALE EYE, AND HIS EARS ARE TIGHT AND SLIGHTLY BACK. THE DOG ON THE LEFT IS THE MORE CONFIDENT IN THIS EXCHANGE. (PHOTO BY LEE PIPER, TAKEN COURTESY OF THE WALKABOUT DOG TRAINING GROUP)

RIGHT: MAI IS SLIGHTLY WORRIED, AS CAN BE SEEN BY THE SET OF HER EARS. IN ADDITION, HER LIPS ARE TIGHT AND FORWARD, AND HER EYE IS EVER SO SLIGHTLY HOODED. (COURTESY PAUL DENTON)

TORAK IS RELAXED; ON THIS OCCASION, HIS BACKWARD-POINTING EARS HAVE NOTHING TO DO WITH HOW HE FEELS: HE IS SIMPLY LISTENING. SOMETIMES, IT'S EASY TO MISINTERPRET THE MESSAGE IF JUST BODY LANGUAGE IS READ: IT'S IMPORTANT TO TAKE INTO ACCOUNT WHAT'S GOING ON AROUND THE ANIMAL AT THE SAME TIME. (COURTESY PATRICK MELTON)

The truth about wolves and dogs

MOSI IS SIMPLY YAWNING HERE. THERE IS NO TENSION IN THE FOREHEAD, HER EYES ARE CLOSED, AND THE EARS, ALTHOUGH BACK, ARE RELAXED. (COURTESY OLIVER MATLA)

A TUCKED TAIL MEANS THE SAME IN WOLVES AS IT DOES IN DOGS: APPREHENSION AND FEAR. (COURTESY CHRIS SENIOR)

A HIGH TAIL CARRIAGE CAN INDICATE THAT A DOG IS CONFIDENT AND AROUSED, THOUGH TAKE CARE TO NOTE WHETHER THE BREED CONCERNED HAS A NATURALLY HIGH TAIL CARRIAGE. (PHOTO BY EMMA COLEMAN, BLINK PHOTOGRAPHY, TAKEN COURTESY OF WALKABOUT DOG TRAINING GROUP)

KODAK IS ALERT AND WEARS AN INTENT LOOK, FOCUSED ON SOMETHING IN FRONT OF HIM. (COURTESY PETE MORGAN LUCAS)

Note, though, that some dogs appear to give off all the right messages, but cannot actually be trusted, whilst others seem very dominant and stiff on approach, but on greeting can be very sociable.

Remember, too, that behaviour breeds behaviour: if your dog rushes into a situation, tries to mount other dogs, or gives conflicting signals, how might the other dog respond? So many previously confident, happy dogs have been frightened by the rude behaviour of other canines, whose owners have allowed them to behave in this anti-social way. They may begin to act in a defensive way, or take the view that it's better to attack first in order to protect themselves.

Be responsible and train your dog to behave politely and properly when he meets other dogs and people, or, at the very least, have your dog under control, and warn others about his reactions, giving them the chance to protect their animals from unwanted and potentially damaging behaviour.

continued page 72

HACKLES CAN BE RAISED (PILOERECTION) OVER THE SHOULDER AREA, JUST THE HIND QUARTERS, OR ALONG THE WHOLE BACK AND TAIL, AND ARE A GOOD INDICATOR OF A CANINE'S MOOD, AS THEY ARE AN INVOLUNTARY RESPONSE. RAISED HACKLES TEND TO INDICATE THAT A DOG IS IN A STATE OF AGGRESSIVE AROUSAL, AND THE MORE AREAS IN WHICH THE HACKLES ARE ERECT, THE MORE AROUSED HE WILL BE, GENERALLY. (COURTESY VICKY ALHADEFF)

The truth about wolves and dogs

LEFT: ALTHOUGH APPEARING DOMINANT WITH A HIGH TAIL CARRIAGE AND RAISED HACKLES, THE REST OF THIS ANIMAL'S BODY HAS A DEFENSIVE POSTURE, WHICH TELLS US HE'S NOT AT ALL SURE ABOUT THE INTERACTION WITH THE OTHER DOG. (COURTESY LEE PIPER)

TORAK (MIDDLE) SHOWING FULL PILOERECTION. (COURTESY PATRICK MELTON)

PILOERECTION IS EVIDENT HERE FROM THE NECK TO MID BACK, AND AGAIN BY THE BASE OF THE TAIL. THIS ANIMAL IS AROUSED ENOUGH TO BEGIN LUNGING AT THE DOG WHO IS STARING AT HIM. (PHOTO BY EMMA COLEMAN, BLINK PHOTOGRAPHY, TAKEN COURTESY OF WALKABOUT DOG TRAINING GROUP)

BEA CAN BE FEARFUL OF PEOPLE, AND TENDS TO REACT BY SHUTTING DOWN, RATHER THAN FIGHTING HER WAY OUT OF SITUATIONS. SHE WILL LOWER HER BODY, SPLAY HER HIND LEGS, AND CLOSE HER EYES. IF THE SITUATION WAS REALLY EXTREME SHE WOULD DROP TO THE GROUND AND URINATE IN FEAR. (COURTESY ANNE CARTER)

The dog in the middle is not happy about the attention from the dogs flanking him: they're only playing but he is feeling threatened. In this sequence, note the changes and signals in his body language, as he tries to convey his feelings about the playful ambush. Note the paw lift, which may be a meta-signal (exaggerated movement to indicate the action is not meant to be aggressive; often seen in rough play, too) intended to communicate his increasing tension, and warning of possible impending aggression. This threat is not carried out, however, as he switches to a more passive fear response when the others fail to back off. (Courtesy Lee Piper)

The truth about wolves and dogs

A classic 'play bow' is an invitation to begin a rough-and-tumble play session.
(Courtesy Vicky Alhadeff)

Other invitations to play include a 'play face,' where the mouth is open and the eyes soft.
(Courtesy Ali Hetherington)

The dog on the left is also trying to start a play session: 'mouthing' and 'jaw fencing' are commonly seen when two dogs interact in a friendly way.
(Courtesy Sarah Harris)

Although it can look quite fearsome, with lots of teeth showing, jaw fencing is a great and safe way for dogs to expend energy and engage in natural behaviour, and wolves jaw fence, too. No harm is done during these sessions, which are either conducted lying down or standing with forefeet off the ground, which means there's no power in the hindquarters. Serious fights between canines are silent with all four paws on the floor. (Courtesy Ali Hetherington)

Play at speed. Dogs will often tuck their tails and charge madly around for a few minutes, often in circles. It's a really good way of expending energy and enticing other dogs to join in the fun! (Courtesy Ali Hetherington)

69

The truth about wolves and dogs

RIGHT: 'PAWING' CAN ALSO INVITE ANOTHER DOG OR WOLF TO PLAY. (COURTESY PATRICK MELTON)

LEFT: A 'NECK GRAB' DURING PLAY IS ALSO COMMON, AND IS NOT A SIGN OF DOMINANCE OR AGGRESSION IN THIS INSTANCE ... (COURTESY LEE PIPER)

... AND WOLVES DO IT, TOO. (COURTESY MONTY SLOAN)

'RIDING UP' ON ANOTHER WOLF OR DOG CAN MEAN MANY THINGS, FROM A THREAT OR RITUALISED ATTACK, TO A GREETING, OR AS A WAY OF SOLICITING PLAY. HERE, THE WOLF ON THE SHOULDERS OF THE OTHER IS IN PLAY MODE: HIS BODY IS RELAXED, TAIL NEUTRAL, AND EYES SOFT. THE WOLF UNDERNEATH HIM IS ALSO VERY RELAXED. (COURTESY OLIVER MATLA)

The truth about wolves and dogs

ON THIS OCCASION, THE SAME BEHAVIOUR HAS A MORE SERIOUS MESSAGE, AS CAN BE SEEN FROM THE RAISED TAIL AND EARS, AND TENSE BODY POSTURE. THE DOG UNDERNEATH IS ALSO SHOWING SIGNS OF DISPLEASURE AND INCREASING DISCOMFORT WHICH COULD ESCALATE INTO AGGRESSION. (COURTESY ALI HETHERINGTON)

Behaviour and instinct

One of the biggest reasons why dog and human relationships break down is because of our lack of awareness of our dogs' instincts, and the need these create in our canine companions. Understand what drives your dog and you can help channel behaviours to suit your lifestyle and expectations.

Dogs come under so much pressure these days: bred for thousands of years to do a specific job, in the modern age they are denied the opportunity to express their natural instincts and work alongside us. So many so-called 'accessory' breeds have fallen foul of fashion, owned by people who know

nothing about – or even care – what the animal needs to live a full and happy life. When, almost inevitably, the dogs are no longer suitable for the role of fashion accessory, they end up, unwanted, in a rescue home, or worse still, are euthanized.

When choosing a dog, make sure you do your research thoroughly, and determine what sort of animal would best fit with the life you can offer it.

Dominance and submission

It may seem confusing to now talk about dominant and submissive body language after trying to convince you that pack hierarchy and the alpha theory is out of date, but I'd like you to come away from the idea of dominant and submissive dogs, and think instead of canine leaders and followers, just as, in the human race, there are those who lead, and those who follow. I hope that, in this way, the aggression normally associated with the idea of dominance, and the notion that our dogs are continually trying to win dominion over us and others, is forever put away, allowing us to see and read the true message and meaning behind the body language of our dogs.

RIGHT: A SUBMISSIVE MUZZLE HOLD. THE LOWER RANKING WOLF APPROACHES THE OTHER IN A LOW, CROUCHED POSITION, AND ACTIVELY SUBMITS BY MUZZLE HOLDING (CAN ALSO INCLUDE MUZZLE LICKING). IF YOUR ADULT DOG DOES THIS, HE IS USING THE SAME GREETING BEHAVIOUR. (COURTESY PATRICK MELTON)

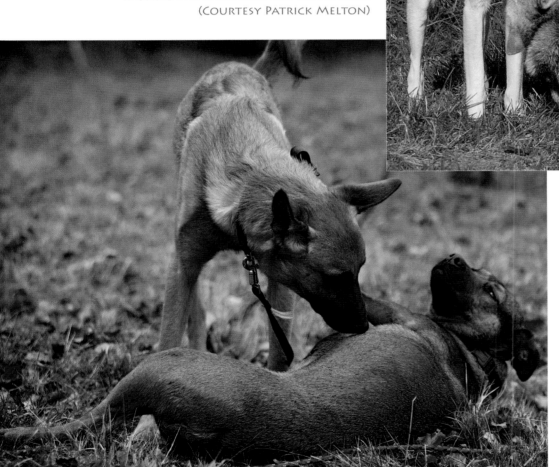

THIS DOG IS PASSIVELY SUBMITTING. CLEARLY, HE WOULD PREFER NOT TO INTERACT AT ALL BUT HAS NO CHOICE IN THE MATTER, SO IS HOPING THAT HIS PASSIVITY WILL CAUSE THE OTHER DOG TO LOSE INTEREST AND MOVE ON. (PHOTO BY EMMA COLEMAN, BLINK PHOTOGRAPHY, TAKEN COURTESY OF WALKABOUT DOG TRAINING GROUP)

IN THE SEQUENCE OVERLEAF THE LONG-HAIRED GERMAN SHEPHERD DOES NOT WANT TO INTERACT WITH THE OTHER DOG, AND SO PASSIVELY SUBMITS BY ROLLING ONTO HER BACK. UNFORTUNATELY, THE POSTURE AND BEHAVIOUR OF THE OTHER DOG INDICATE THAT HE HAS NOT RESPONDED TO HER CALMING SIGNALS. AFTER ALLOWING HIM TO SCENT HER, THE FEMALE BEGINS TO RISE AND THEN FLIPS INTO FEARFUL DEFENSIVE BEHAVIOUR. (PHOTO BY LEE PIPER, TAKEN COURTESY OF WALKABOUT DOG TRAINING GROUP)

The truth about wolves and dogs

THE YOUNG, BOISTEROUS BLACK DOG IS ONLY PLAYING, BUT THE DOG UNDERNEATH, AFTER PASSIVELY SUBMITTING, HAS BECOME EXTREMELY ANXIOUS. HE HAS TENSED UP AND WILL EVENTUALLY BEGIN TO USE HIS LEGS AND PAWS TO PUSH THE RUDE YOUNGER DOG OFF HIM AND AWAY. (PHOTO BY EMMA COLEMAN BLINK PHOTOGRAPHY, TAKEN COURTESY OF WALKABOUT DOG TRAINING GROUP)

The truth about wolves and dogs

THE BLACK WOLF IS DISPLAYING SUBMISSIVE BEGGING. CUBS WILL COMMONLY DISPLAY THIS BEHAVIOUR, BUT ADULT WOLVES WILL ALSO USE IT AS A WAY OF SECURING FOOD FROM A HIGHER RANKING INDIVIDUAL. (COURTESY PATRICK MELTON)

How to have a happy dog

The truth about wolves and dogs

Imagine the following scenario. You are an intelligent, energetic person who has a talent for computer programming, which you love with a passion: it's what you live for. You want to write programmes all the time, as doing this would make you happy and proud.

The only problem is that you hardly ever get to do it! You are stuck at home alone all day with a computer you are not allowed to use. When the rest of your family get home at night they do not greet you on arrival, but tell you off when you try to interact with them, which you do really enthusiastically, as you have been bored and lonely.

Sometimes your family goes straight out again without you or, because you are boisterous and ask too many questions, or plead to go on the computer, they shut you in another room on your own – again! If visitors call, no-one wants to talk to you about computers, so again you are excluded. Then you have to watch as everyone else in the house has a go on the

computer while you patiently wait your turn. Finally, you're allowed a go, but only very briefly, and aren't able to finish what you started; the computer is switched off before you've even had a chance to save your work. You protest but this gets you nowhere except being excluded again, or, even worse, you are physically dragged away from the computer by your shirt collar, kicking and screaming in frustration and fear.

Sometimes, your family does take you with them when they go out, but you are often left in the car while the others have fun at a computer fair. At home, your favourite family member gives you their full attention for only about half an hour a day, and the rest of the time – if not alone – you are ignored or teased by younger family members. In the evenings, you are just beginning to settle and enjoy the attention and affection of your favourite family member when everyone goes to bed, leaving you alone – again. Your bedroom is downstairs, far away from your family. If they hear you crying in the night

DOGS LOVE TO BE OUT AND ABOUT WITH THEIR CANINE AND HUMAN FRIENDS. (COURTESY ANNE CARTER)

because you feel sad and afraid you are told off, and threatened with being disowned.

After months, even years, of this abuse, you try to use the computer while the rest of the family is out, but you accidentally break it, getting you into even more trouble. In the end you are so frustrated and emotionally distressed you lash out at one of the family who is teasing you, and hurt them, and are thrown out onto the streets as a result.

Improbable? Maybe, but not if you substitute the average pet dog for the person in this story. Pack animals – be they wolf, dog or human – are all highly social beings that thrive on companionship, affection, and the reassurance of living in a secure group. One of the biggest rewards you can give a wolf is the company of others, and your dog is no different in this respect.

Lack of mental stimulus can be very stressful. We've all had a job that didn't provide us with sufficient stimulus and challenge: remember how that made you feel: bored; frustrated; unfulfilled. Well, your canine companion at home alone all day is experiencing those very same emotions. Now think of

ALLOWING DOGS TO USE THEIR NATURAL ABILITIES BY CHANNELLING THEM INTO APPROPRIATE ACTIVITIES CAN BE REALLY SATISFYING FOR BOTH YOU AND YOUR DOG. DESIGN GAMES WHICH USE THEIR INNATE SKILLS: NOSEWORK, RETRIEVING, EVEN HERDING INSTINCTS, CAN BE SATISFIED WITH THE RIGHT GAMES, THEREBY REDUCING THE POSSIBLITY THAT YOUR CANINE FRIEND WILL FIND LESS SOCIALLY ACCEPTABLE WAYS OF 'WORKING.' (COURTESY ALI HETHERINGTON)

The truth about wolves and dogs

MENTAL STIMULUS IS JUST AS IMPORTANT AS PHYSICAL EXERCISE, AND DOGS LOVE TO LEARN. DOING A SMALL AMOUNT OF OBEDIENCE TRAINING WHILST ON YOUR WALK CAN ENGAGE YOUR DOG AND IMPROVE YOUR HANDLING ABILITIES. (COURTESY ANNE CARTER)

the best job you ever had, or a favourite sport at which you excel. How does that make you feel? Do you think your dog is happy and satisfied with a fast trot around the block, without being able to stop even once to sniff a street lamp? Or being allowed to run free for an hour, but on his own – again –

without any interaction from you? Think: what did my dog get out of that? Is he mentally as well as physically sated? Did he *enjoy* that?

People and animals need mental and physical stimulation. Many dogs from working breeds never get to use their innate instincts, and so they go

USUALLY FULL OF FUN, DOGS LOVE IT IF YOU ARE, TOO! PLAYING WITH THEM IN NOVEL WAYS CAN EXCITE AND STIMULATE THEM.
(COURTESY ANNE CARTER)

'self-employed.' I have seen gun dogs 'retrieving' books from shelves, quietly handing them to their owners. Herding dogs often round up children, nipping them on the ankles to get them to move faster. Guard dogs protect bits of paper – the list is endless.

If you can allow your dog to work, or have something to do, he will be so much happier: there's no shortage of activities that you can both get involved in. Get out and enjoy your dog having fun: chances are you'll enjoy yourself, too! When you cannot give him your full attention safe, interactive toys and chews are an acceptable substitute for a time, and the bigger the variety, the better. Some dogs need to have their toys rotated (put away for a while and then reintroduced to retain their interest in them), whilst others have a favourite that they always choose to play with.

It's instinctive for dogs to chew and use their jaws, which, in the wild is facilitated by chewing bones from prey. Some dogs will chew out of nervousness: a bit like us biting our fingernails. Whatever the reason, dogs need this jaw exercise and the mental stimulus it provides so ensure your dog receives plenty of both in an appropriate form: ie not a chair leg. This chewing activity is not intended to be a replacement for interaction with you and those of his own kind, but at times when you are busy and he has to entertain himself, it's a good second-best.

Dogs can never have too many toys or appropriate objects to chew and nibble on, which not only provides mental stimulus but works their jaw, too, something modern food rarely does. (Courtesy Shanon McAuliffe)

All breeds have innate instincts, and the trick is to channel these in the right direction, to preclude the possibility of your dog displaying these inappropriately – and getting into trouble for doing so ... (Courtesy Shanon McAuliffe)

LABRADOR PUPPIES ROLO AND RUBY ARE ALREADY SHOWING SIGNS OF A GOOD GUNDOG RETRIEVE.
(COURTESY ANNE CARTER)

The truth about wolves and dogs

Pick the right breed/crossbreed for you and your lifestyle

One way to increase your chances of a suitable match between you and your dog is to throughly research the breed or mixture of breeds you are considering *before* you welcome a dog into your life. For example, it's a bad idea to buy a collie if your idea of exercising is a gentle stroll in the park. A collie will require a great deal of mental and physical stimulation, and may well attempt to provide his own if he doesn't get this from you – with possibly dire consequences.

Sometimes, dogs are chosen because their new owner likes how they look, without knowing anything about the breed's temperament or instinctual behaviour. They're surprised when their sweet little terrier grows up and takes up hunting when out on a walk, often running off for an hour at a time. Know the breed before you choose your dog: exercise levels, grooming requirements, attitude to strangers and other animals, potential health problems, the breed's 'job.' Can you replicate that purpose? Of course, not all collies herd sheep, but do you have the time to take yours to agility or fly ball classes to provide the stimulus he needs?

The Guide Dogs for the Blind Association always considers these points when matching a dog with a new owner, knowing that an energetic Labrador should not be paired with an older person who doesn't get out and about a great deal. A Labrador with boundless energy needs a fit, active owner who walks at the fast pace the breed needs and likes. They complement one another.

When offering a home to a dog, carefully consider how you live, work and play. A Pekingese may not be the best choice if you're off hill walking most weekends, and a Rhodesian Ridgeback is not for someone with a fairly sedentary lifestyle. The many available informative breed books and internet websites can provide all the info you need to make an informed choice, so do your homework, and talk to people who already own the breed you are considering, or rescue societies.

And if you already own a dog but don't know much about him, it's never too late to learn: a few simple changes to your lifestyle and how you manage your dog can make a world of difference to you both. When discussing the problems he was having with his dog, an owner told me that he "... just wanted a dog," and did not want to devote the time required to deal with any issues that having a dog might throw up. My response to this? Dogs are not objects that you can pick up and put down at will. They are intelligent, sentient animals that need your time, patience, understanding and love.

DOGS LOVE THE COMPANY AND MENTAL STIMULUS OF BEING WITH OTHERS OF THEIR OWN KIND. IF YOU ARE A SINGLE DOG FAMILY, MAKING THE EFFORT TO MEET UP WITH OTHER WELL SOCIALISED DOGS CAN REALLY MAKE A DIFFERENCE TO YOUR DOG'S LIFE. PLAY IS SO IMPORTANT. (COURTESY ALI HETHERINGTON)

LEFT: SOME DOGS WILL WELCOME ANOTHER CANINE IN THE HOUSE AND STRIKE UP A STRONG RELATIONSHIP ... (COURTESY KAREN BUSH)

... WHILST OTHERS ARE HAPPY WITH THEIR HUMAN FAMILY FOR COMPANY. SINGHA IS DREAMING OF WORLD DOMINATION, OBVIOUSLY: WHY ELSE WOULD SHE BE CUDDLED UP WITH HER DAD? (COURTESY SHANON McAULIFFE)

Companionship

One of the easiest ways to ensure that yours is a happy dog is to provide the company he will crave. Some dogs prefer that company to be other dogs, some their owners, or at least another person. Whichever form of companionship is provided, there must be enough of it.

I have often had clients ask me for advice about various problems they are experiencing with their dogs, and it transpires that their work pattern is twelve hour shifts. This usually means that they are out of the house for thirteen hours straight, and if they sleep the average eight hours a night, their dog receives a maximum of just three hours' company a day. Result? One very stressed and lonely dog.

Meeting needs

Owning a dog is a big commitment and not one that should be taken lightly. In trying to decide whether you can offer a dog a good home, and a happy and fulfilled life with you, it may be helpful to ask yourself the following questions, which are presented in no particular order of importance:

✔ Will I be able to provide the company he needs?
✔ Can I take my dog on holiday with me, or provide suitable care for him if not?
✔ Who will look after him while I'm at work, or can I take him with me?
✔ Can I afford a dog sitter/walker?
✔ Do I have a time-consuming hobby, and can he join in?
✔ Will my friends and family be happy for him to visit them?
✔ Can I provide him with some doggy friends with whom he can regularly play?
✔ Is my car/vehicle suitable for him to travel safely in?
✔ Can I include him in all aspects of my family life?
✔ Can I provide him with the daily nourishment that he needs?
✔ Am I prepared to exercise him regularly, even when the weather is inclement?
✔ Am I able to afford the veterinary care required, such as annual vaccinations, plus any other treatment he may require?
✔ Do I have the time to devote to his welfare, such as proper grooming, checking him over bodily?
✔ Am I prepared for the impact he will have on my home – furniture, etc – and the extra work involved in clearing up after him?

If you answer 'no' more often than 'yes' to the above questions, you should resolve to change your lifestyle to accommodate a dog, or perhaps reconsider having one at all.

I used to have the perfect lifestyle for my first dog, Buzz. I worked for Guide Dogs for the Blind, so he was able to come to work with me, and could usually be found in the office being greeted by all and sundry. There were other dogs in the office, and at lunchtime they played together. At the end of the day, Buzz had me all to himself.

At weekends I was out on the canal or river boating, and Buzz would either trot along the towpath beside me, 'helping' at all the locks, or run up and down the roof of the boat. We stopped in new and exciting places each night, met loads of dogs and people during the day, and went to the pub in the

WITH THE RIGHT VEHICLE AND THE CORRECT EQUIPMENT TO KEEP HIM SAFE, YOUR DOG CAN TRAVEL WITH YOU TO EXPLORE NEW PLACES. (COURTESY ANNE CARTER)

evening. He would come in to town to visit friends, go on group walks, travel home with me to see my parents, and to other Guide Dog centres if I was working away, or stay with friends if he could not go with me.

When I did have to leave Buzz alone at home for a few hours, he was quite happy because he was relaxed and tired, as I would always make sure he had had a good run before I left. On top of all this I would play with him, teach him tricks, and let him sleep in my bedroom. He was the perfect dog and we had a brilliant relationship. I was lucky to be able to fairly easily give him all he needed, something I find much harder to achieve today with my present dog, given my different working commitments.

Dogs love nothing more than being part of the family. Social inclusion is a fundamental need in all canines: do this and they will thrive.

Be mindful of what you think, feel, and do

Much has been written about the qualities of a good dog trainer, but what effect our emotions and thoughts have on our dogs is not usually mentioned. I believe that the power of intent (the emotion behind an action) is profound and, together with the aforementioned psychological factors, differentiate a good trainer/owner from a great one. It has already been established that dogs have perfected the art of 'reading' our faces and the emotions they portray, which makes it very hard to fool our canine friends as they glean our innermost feelings and react to them accordingly.

In fact, some canines are so perceptive it almost seems as if they have that sixth sense, extra sensory perception (ESP), although once the true extent of canine awareness is appreciated, it becomes obvious that they possess all they need to interpret our behaviour. Dogs have such an extraordinary sense of smell, for example, and can discern our emotions via the pheromones we give off. Take some of the following examples of this.

Numerous incidents over the years have convinced me that canines are amazing emotional barometers, which we can use to our advantage, although it has been known to backfire. My first dog – Buzz – had really good recall. Occasionally, this would go awry, and he would take ages to return, running in big circles and sniffing, as I waited, becoming more and more irritated. However, I came to realise that the only days he would do this were when I was already in a bad mood, in a hurry, or upset about something. Once I became aware of this and dropped the emotion, he would come running to me. Buzz had been giving me calming signals by not coming back because he felt wary of approaching me, and was waiting until my mental state was

CANINES NATURALLY LOVE EXPLORING NEW ENVIRONMENTS, SO WALKING YOUR DOG IN THE SAME PLACE EVERY DAY CAN BE VERY DULL, AND GIVE RISE TO ISSUES CAUSED BY BOREDOM. (COURTESY ANNE CARTER)

89

The truth about wolves and dogs

DOGS CAN TAKE PART IN MANY FAMILY ACTIVITIES AND HOBBIES. HOWEVER, IF YOU TAKE YOUR DOG RUNNING AND CYCLING WITH YOU, ENSURE THAT HE IS FIT ENOUGH, AND ACTUALLY WANTS TO PARTICIPATE. IN A SAFE ENVIRONMENT IT'S FAR PREFERABLE FOR A DOG TO BE OFF-LEAD WHEN TAKING PART IN THESE HIGH ENERGY ACTIVITIES, BECAUSE AT LEAST THEN HE CAN CHOOSE WHEN TO SLOW DOWN IF TIRED, AND ALSO INDULGE IN NATURAL BEHAVIOUR SUCH AS SNIFFING AND SCENT-MARKING, WHICH WOULDN'T BE POSSIBLE WHILST ON THE MOVE. THERE'S ALSO LESS DANGER THAT YOUR BIKE AND YOUR DOG WILL COME INTO CONTACT WITH POSSIBLY TRAGIC RESULTS. (PHOTO BY EMMA COLEMAN, BLINK PHOTOGRAPHY, TAKEN COURTESY OF WALKABOUT DOG TRAINING GROUP)

such that he felt happy to return. Looking at my dog and seeing how he was responding to me let me see what my mental and emotional states were.

Animals pick up so much from us by appearing to tune in to our thoughts and feelings. I cannot count the number of times I have wondered where my cat is, only for him to hop though the cat flap a few minutes later: it's happened too often for it to be a fluke. Of course, this also seems to work in a negative way: how many of us have decided that it's time to bath our dog, only to find he's disappeared, or is hiding behind the sofa? Our dogs somehow know the minute we are about to stand up to fetch the lead and take them for a walk, get their supper dish out and prepare their food, take them to the vet, and even the difference between ruffling their coat and applying a spot-on parasitic treatment!

I knew a dog that could tell his own homeopathic treatment bottle from others: if any of these were selected there was no reaction, but if his bottle was picked up, he ran away. The intent – to give him his medicine – was overwhelming, and he fled. Our agenda to do what has to be done is so strong, and our attention so focused on it, that dogs – sensitive, perceptive creatures that they are – are bound to pick up on the changes in posture, breath rate, sense of purpose and energy that we exhibit at such times. And if they don't like what's coming, they make themselves scarce!

Intent can play a huge role in how dogs react to us. Occasionally, I have worked with dogs that initially react negatively when I begin Tellington TTouch with them, and this is because I am thinking about and focusing on the dog too much, and he simply cannot cope with the attention. When this happens, I turn the session into a game to lighten the atmosphere, and they soon respond positively.

I believe that the foregoing demonstrates how what appear to be behavioural problems can so often be attributed to us and our inner state. If you are unsure about or actually scared of something, our dogs are more likely to have a problem about the cause as well. I've even known dogs show aggression or dislike toward a person that their owner did not like. Or it could be that the dislike was mutual between the two individuals, and the dog had picked up on this.

The truth about wolves and dogs

If you find yourself and your dog in a situation that you think he may be fearful of, projecting a calm, unbothered approach can really help, as he will see that you are not worried, and understand that there is no reason for him to be either. Holding our breath and casting anxious glances at our dog when we hear the first firework of the season will only convince him that he has reason to worry about the noise.

One of the wolves I used to work with is highly suspicious of new objects in her environment, and will panic if asked to walk past them. If her handler stays very matter of fact, gives no eye contact or reassurance, she will, after a quick check in with the handler, walk past the object concerned. It's not cruel to apparently disregard her fears but simply saying: "I am a confident, authoritative figure and this situation does not bother me."

Another example which Golden Retriever owners may be familiar with is overdoing the sympathy when their dog is ill. I have cared for many sick Golden Retrievers in my time working for Guide Dogs, and if I spoke to them in a sad, overly-sympathetic voice I could see them physically sinking into themselves and giving up. By being upbeat, they would respond in kind and recover much more quickly.

And relax ...
(Courtesy Emma
Coleman, Blink
Photography)

93

When training dogs I always try to hold in my mind a picture of what it is I'd like them to do when I ask them to do it. Giving the verbal command helps me to picture the behaviour I want and enables my body to give the correct signals.

For example, when working dogs through Tellington TTouch groundwork exercises, I often ask: "Can you take two steps for me?" and they usually do! It's instinctive for us to picture what we're talking about, or asking for, in our minds, so if we ask our dog to put all four feet on the ground, chances are he will comply. The picture is projected – the thought is out there.

Being a great trainer is not about an individual's size or strength, and neither does it come from a book or a qualification, although they are both good places to start. Experience, inner strength, the ability to project a calm, almost aloof, matter-of-fact confidence, be flexible and not hold on to an unachievable objective, are the qualities that go toward making a great trainer. Most of all it's working with your dog and understanding that emotions and intent can play as big a role in influencing behaviour as any physical training methods you may use.

Say 'no' to inappropriate training methods

Probably only you know your dog intimately. By all means read a hundred books and talk with countless trainers, but, at the end of the day, you must make your own decisions about what is best for you and your dog.

Dog trainers are not infallible, they don't have all the answers, and can even create problems through inappropriate handling or management of a training class or session. Don't be afraid to ask questions of them: what are their qualifications? Where did they learn to train? Watch them work with a dog: do they have empathy; can they adapt their methods to suit the dog's needs; what do they do if a dog does not seem to understand the lesson they are teaching? Do they blame the dog when they fail? How does the dog react?

Is the dog apparently doing what is asked of him but also showing stress behaviour, or is he willingly doing as asked and enjoying the session? Is he allowed to express how he is feeling without fear of reprimand or punishment? Dogs bark, growl or cower for a reason; it's how they express themselves. If this expression is denied them, how can they tell us how they feel?

Go with your gut instinct when deciding what is right for you and your dog and it will rarely let you down. Above all, 'think dog,' try to view the world from his perspective, and acknowledge his ancestry and need to express himself, and be heard – in today's ultra-busy world.

We have been taught that we must control every aspect of our dog's life, and through this have denied him free expression, which surely is the right of every living creature? And all in the name of the incorrect and outdated concept that all dogs are trying to assert authority over us.

Let's have a revolution and let our dogs *be* dogs. Let them be our faithful companions, acknowledge and welcome the fact that they have thoughts, feelings and a right to express themselves, just as we do.

"WHEN I GROW UP I'D LIKE TO READ – I MEAN RETRIEVE – THE NEWSPAPER." (COURTESY ANNE CARTER)

Appendices

Tellington TTouch training (TTouch) around the world

TTouch in Australia
www.listeningtowhispers.com

TTouch in Austria
www.tteam.at

TTouch in Belgium
www.ttouch.be

TTouch in Canada
5435 Rochdell Road
Vernon, BC V1B 3E8
Tel: 250-545-2336
Fax: 250-545-9116
www.tteam-ttouch.ca

TTouch in England
Tilley Farm
Timsbury Road
Farmborough
Bath BA2 0AB
www.ttouchtteam.co.uk

Toni Shelbourne – www.tellingtontouch.co.uk

TTouch in France
Lisa Leicht – lisa@lisaleicht.ch
Bibi Degn – bibi@tteam.de

TTouch in Germany
www.tteam.de

TTouch in Ireland
www.ttouchtteam-ireland.com

TTouch in Italy
www.tteam.it

TTouch in Japan
www.ttouch.jp

Touch in The Netherlands
www.tteam-ttouch.nl

References & sources

Erb F H Jr, *How to Train Dogs and Cats*. Published in 1904 by Jennings & Graham, Chicago

Hammond S T, *Practical Dog Training: or Training versus Breaking*. Published in 1882 by Forest and Stream Publishing Co

Hartley O, *Hunting Dogs*. Published in 1909 by A R Harding Publishing Co

Haberlein E F, *The Amateur Trainer, Force System without the Whip*. Published in 1895 by Ketcheson A Reeves, Leavenworth, Kansas

Hutchinson, Major General W N *Dog Breaking*. Published in 1865 by John Murray Publishing, Albemarle Street, London

Richardson, Lieutenant Colonel E H *British War Dogs Their Training and Psychology*. Published in 1920 by Skeffington & Son Ltd, London.

Schenkei R. Expression Study on Wolves, Captivity Observations. 1946

Waters B, *Modern Training & Handling*. Published in 1894 by J Loring Thayer Publishing Co

Mech, L D 1999. Alpha status, dominance, and division of labor in wolf packs. Canadian Journal of Zoology 77:1196-1203.

Genetic Structure of the Purebred Domestic Dog: Heidi G Parker, Lisa V Kim, Nathan B Sutter, Scott Carlson, Travis D Lorentzen, Tiffany B Malek, Gary S Johnson, Hawkins B DeFrance, Elaine. Ostrander and Leonid Kruglyak, 2004, published in Science V304 www.sciencemag.org

Regarding the quotes in chapter three from gundog training books, to my knowledge they are all out of copyright. I have tried to trace present owners of the works, but, as most of the publishers no longer exist, this has been challenging, to say the least.

The truth about wolves and dogs

TTouch Events in New Zealand
www.listeningtowhispers.com

TTouch in Slovenia
Darja Slovenija
www.ranckajaingrom.com

TTouch in South Africa
www.ttouch.co.za

TTouch in Spain
Bibi Degn – bibi@tteam.de

TTouch in Sweden
Christina Drangel – jmpette@ibm.net

TTouch in Switzerland
www.tellingtonttouch.ch

TTouch in USA
1713 State Rd 502
Santa Fe, NM 87506
Tel: 866-4-TTouch (866-488-6824)
Fax: 505-455-7233
www.tellingtontouch.com

Specialist care

Acupressure (worldwide)
www.animalacupressure.com

American Holistic Veterinary Medical Association (USA)
www.ahvma.org

American Veterinary Chiropractic Association (USA)
www.animalchiropractic.org

Association of British Veterinary Acupuncturists
www.abva.co.uk

Association of Chartered Physiotherapists in Animal Therapy (UK)
www.acpat.org

British Association of Homeopathic Veterinary Surgeons
www.bahvs.com

British Association of Veterinary Herbalists
www.herbalvets.org.uk

Greyfriars Rehabilitation and Hydrotherapy Centre
Surrey, England
www.greyfriarsrehab.co.uk

International Veterinary Acupuncture Society
www.ivas.org

International Veterinary Chiropractic Association
www.ivca.de

McTimoney Animal Association (UK)
www.mctimoney-animal.org.uk

McTimoney Chiropractor Association (UK)
www.mctimoneychiropractic.org

National Association of Registered Canine Hydrotherapists
www.narch.org.uk

Veterinary Botanical Medical Association (USA)
www.vbma.org

(COURTESY OLIVER MATLA)

(COURTESY ANNE CARTER)

Wolf organisations

International Wolf Centre (US)
www.wolf.org

www.davemech.org
www.mnforsustain.org/wolf_mech_
dominance_alpha_status.htm (founder of IWC)

UK Wolf Conservation Trust
www.ukwolf.org

Wolf Park (US)
www.wolfpark.org

Alternative Practitioners/information

Canine Health Concern
www.canine-health-concern.org.uk

Naturally Happy Dogs
www.naturallyhappydogs.com - natural-directory

The truth about wolves and dogs

Taranet – Complementary Animal Therapies Directory
www.taranet.co.uk

Main wolf projects supported by the UK Wolf Conservation Trust (UKWCT)

(For more information visit www.ukwolf.org/projects)

Balkani Wildlife Society (large carnivore centre, Bulgaria)
www.balkani.org

Ethiopian Wolf Conservation Programme
www.ethiopianwolf.org

Mexican Wolf Fund
www.californiawolfcenter.org

Red Wolf Coalition, NC USA
www.redwolves.com

Wolf management in Croatia
www.life-vuk.hr

Photography
Monty Sloan – www.wolfphotography.com
Oliver Matla – www.lupinity.com

Environmental education

Education 4 Conservation
www.education4conservation.org

Further reading

Canine Behaviour A Photo Illustrated Handbook by Barbara Handelman, M Ed, CDBC
Wolf Ethogram published by Wolf Park www.wolfpark.org
Wolves: Ecology, Behaviour and Conservation by L David Mech and Luigi Boitani
Dog Speak – recognising and understanding behaviour by Christiane Blenski, published by Hubble and Hattie

Life Skills for Puppies: laying the foundation for a loving, lasting relationship by Helen Zulch and Daniel Mills, published by Hubble and Hattie
Getting in TTouch with your Dog by Linda Tellington Jones
Unlock Your Dog's Potential: How to Achieve a Calm and Happy Canine by Sarah Fisher
100 Ways to Train the Perfect Dog by Sarah Fisher & Marie Miller
100 Ways to Solve Your Dog's Problems by Sarah Fisher & Marie Miller

General training

Association of Pet Dog Trainers (Australia)
www.apdt.com.au

Association of Pet Dog Trainers (UK)
www.apdt.co.uk

Association of Pet Dog Trainers (USA)
www.apdt.com

Clicker training

Karen Pryor - US
www.clickertraining.com

Activities to do with your dog

Agility
(an obstacle course done at speed)
www.agilitynet.co.uk
www.usdaa.com (American dog agility association)

Breed showing
www.thekennelclub.org.uk/dogshowing
www.akc.org USA

Cani-Cross
(running with your dog)
www.cani-cross.co.uk
www.cani-cross.eu/website

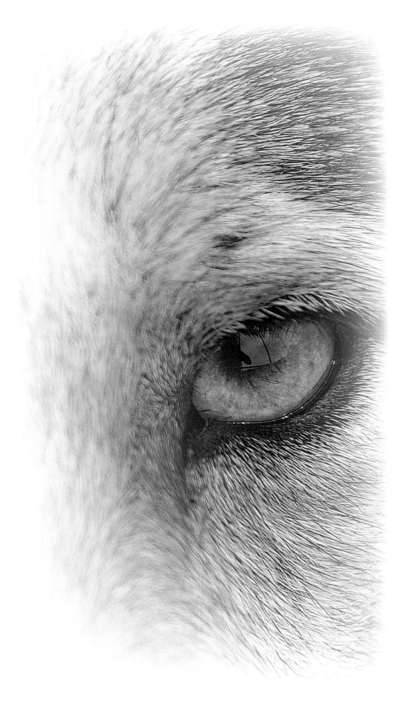

Competition Obedience
www.obedienceuk.com

Dog Scurry
(a competition designed from gundog activities; usually held at country shows)
www.scurrybandits.org

Flyball
(dogs compete in a relay race to retrieve balls from a dispenser. Smaller dogs can play flymouse, in which the tennis play is replaced by a soft toy)
www.flyball.org.uk

Heelwork to music – dancing with your dog
www.heelworktomusic.co.uk

National Association of Dog Obedience Instructors USA
www.nadoi.org

Rally Obedience
(a competitive sport where the handler and dog have to negotiate a course of various activities)

Treibball
(a new sport where dogs herd large exercise balls. Popular in the Netherlands, Germany and the USA. Very new to the UK)
www.americantreibballassociation.org

Working Trials
(a sport in which your dog develops similar skills to those of police dogs. Involves obedience, tracking, agility, fitness, etc)
www.thekennelclub.org.uk/workingtrials

For information on traditional activities for working dogs visit
www.countrymanfairs.co.uk

(COURTESY CHRIS SENIOR)

The truth about wolves and dogs

BEA CAME TO LIVE WITH ME IN JANUARY 2012, AFTER BEING TAKEN IN BY THE LABRADOR LIFELINE TRUST THE PREVIOUS NOVEMBER. SHE WAS SO TRAUMATISED AND FEARFUL, THE TRUST ASKED ME TO WORK WITH HER. I VISITED HER WEEKLY AND WE MADE GREAT PROGRESS. BY JANUARY 2012 SHE WAS READY TO FACE THE WORLD, AND CAME TO ME INITIALLY AS A FOSTER: I ADOPTED HER A FEW MONTHS LATER.

BEA IS TESTAMENT TO POSITIVE TRAINING AND THE NEED FOR PATIENCE AND UNDERSTANDING. AS PART OF THE PHYSICAL AND MENTAL ABUSE SHE SUFFERED, SHE MUST HAVE BEEN HARSHLY TRAINED, AS COMMON COMMANDS SUCH AS 'SIT' WOULD SEND HER INTO A BLIND PANIC. AFTER MONTHS OF CONFIDENCE-BUILDING SHE IS NOW LEARNING

TO LOVE THE MENTAL STIMULUS OF TRAINING, ALTHOUGH I HAVE HAD TO CHANGE ALL THE USUAL COMMAND WORDS. SHE WILL ALWAYS BEAR THE EMOTIONAL SCARS OF HER PREVIOUS LIFE, BUT WITH ME IS A LOVING, TRUSTING, BEAUTIFUL DOG. SHE TEACHES ME SOMETHING EVERY DAY AS I HAVE TO RETHINK EVERYTHING I DO WHEN HANDLING HER, ANTICIPATING HER FEARS AND ANXIETIES. (AUTHOR COLLECTION)

INDEX

The truth about wolves and dogs

Visit Hubble and Hattie on the web: www.hubbrandhattie.com and www.hubbleandhattie • blogspot.com
f twitter • Details of all books • Special offers • Newsletter • New book news

104

Essential reading: before you bring home your new puppy, READ THIS BOOK!

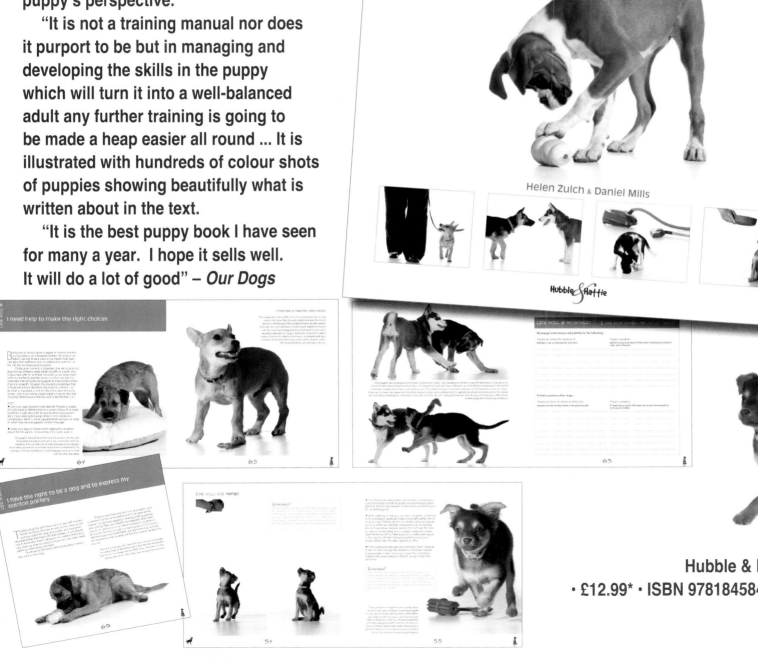

LIFE SKILLS FOR PUPPIES

Laying the foundation for a loving, lasting relationship

Helen Zulch & Daniel Mills

Hubble & Hattie

Hubble & Hattie
• £12.99* • ISBN 9781845844462

"I just don't know what my dog wants from me!"

If you feel like this at times, then THIS is the book for you!

Dogs use their whole body to communicate –teeth, ears, tail. eyes, fur, posture – and this book explains in a straightforward, jargon-free way the meaning behind this body language.

Learn to pay attention to your dog's signals and interpret them correctly, and *really* undertand what it is your dog is saying to you!

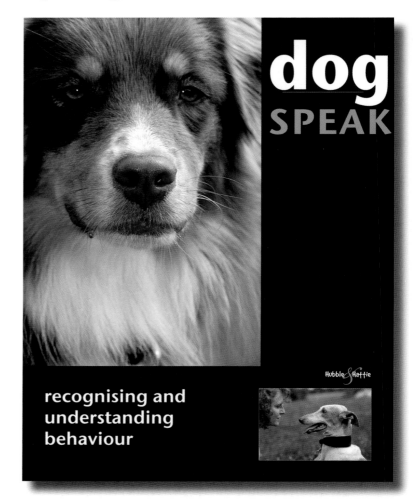

dog SPEAK

recognising and understanding behaviour

Hubble & Hattie

Ready, set, PLAY!

"... a really good read for all dog owners" – Pet Magazine

"... the end result is a tried-and-tested mood lifter for you and your dog" – Dogs NSW

Christiane Blenski

Dog Games

Stimulating play to entertain your dog and you

Hubble & Hattie

Hubble & Hattie · £15.99* · ISBN 9781845843328

the complete dog massage manual

Julia Robertson

Hubble & Hattie

Gentle Dog Care

swim to recovery
canine hydrotherapy healing

Hubble & Hattie

Emily Wong

Gentle Dog Care

living with an older dog

David Alderton & Derek Hall

Hubble & Hattie

Photographs by Marc Henrie,
with additional material from Derek Hall

Gentl

"... a visually appealing and useful book" – Dog Training Weekly

Hubble & Hattie • £12.99*
• ISBN 9781845843571

"... a choice and very highly recommended read for dog lovers, a resource not to be missed" – Midwest Book Review

Hubble & Hattie • £12.99*
• ISBN 9781845843359

exercising your puppy
a gentle & natural approach

Hubble & Hattie

Julia Robertson &
Elisabeth Pope

Gentle Dog Care

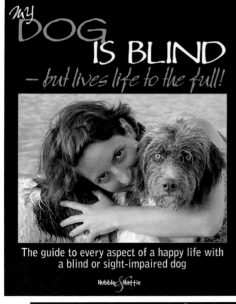

£9.99* each

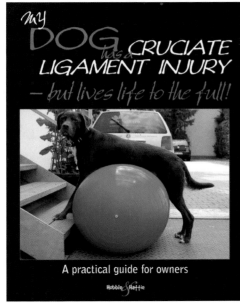

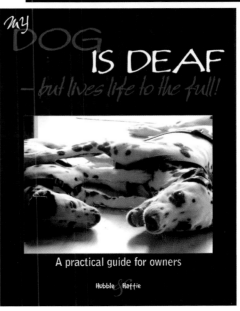

"... aims to empower owners and allow them to develop a sensitivity to, and an understanding of a very distressing condition" (My dog is blind) – Veterinary Record

"A fine and much recommended pick for any dog owner facing this all-too-common problem ...." (My dog is deaf) – Midwest Book Review

"... sensible, down-to-earth tips abound ... the photos I found fascinating ..." (My dog has hip dysplasia) – Trevor Turner BVetMed, MRCVS, FRSH, MCIArb

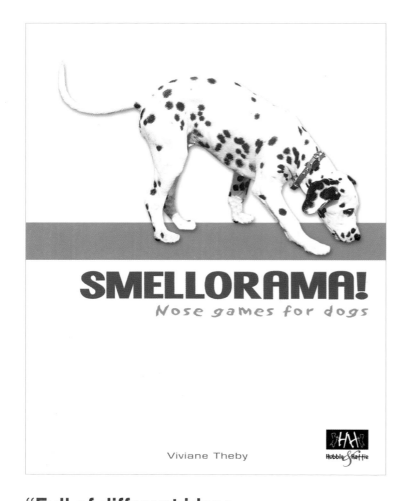

SMELLORAMA!
Nose games for dogs

Viviane Theby

EMERGENCY FIRST AID FOR DOGS

At home and away